The Cortisol D... Diet Plan

The Ultimate Guide to Manage Stress, Balance Hormones, and Transform Your Body. 30-day Meal Plan Included.

Amanda Willson

Table of Contents

Introduction: Understanding Cortisol and How Diet Can Help

What Is Cortisol?

To be very honest, stress is a given in life. Our bodies are in an almost continual state of go, go, go from the time we wake up to a screaming alarm clock to the continuous alerts on our phones. And central to this stress reaction is? One hormone known as cortisol.

With good cause, cortisol is sometimes referred to as the stress hormone. Your adrenal glands generate it, and it is absolutely vital for maintaining alertness, controlling inflammation, and even metabolic regulation.

In short, it's not the enemy—it's actually trying to help you.

Think of cortisol as your body's built-in alarm system. When you face a stressful situation, your brain sends a signal to your adrenal glands to release cortisol, which in turn gives you the energy and focus needed to deal with the challenge. Back in the days when our ancestors had to outrun wild animals, this system was life-saving.

But in today's world, we're not running from lions—we're running from deadlines, bills, sleepless nights, and never-ending to-do lists. Instead of occasional cortisol spikes (which are normal), many of us are stuck in a chronic state of high cortisol. And when cortisol stays high for too long, it starts to take a toll on the body in ways we might not even realize.

How High Cortisol Affects Your Body and Mind

If you've been feeling constantly **tired but wired**, struggling with stubborn belly fat, or noticing that you snap at little things that never used to bother you, cortisol might be playing a bigger role in your life than you think.

When cortisol levels remain elevated for an extended period, it can lead to:

- **Weight gain -** especially around the belly—cortisol tells your body to save fat, mostly around the stomach, as a survival tactic.

- **Poor sleep** – High cortisol levels can make it difficult to fall asleep or stay asleep, leading to that dreaded cycle of exhaustion and restlessness.

- **Increased anxiety and irritability** – Ever feel like the smallest things set you off? High cortisol can make you feel on edge and emotionally drained.

- **Digestive issues** – Your gut and brain are closely linked, and too much cortisol can lead to bloating, acid reflux, or IBS-like symptoms.

- **Blood sugar imbalances** – Cortisol increases blood sugar levels, which can lead to energy crashes and intense sugar cravings.

- **Weakened immune function** – If you find yourself getting sick more often, it could be because chronic stress is suppressing your immune system.

And perhaps the most frustrating part? **It's not just about stress.** Certain foods, lack of sleep, excessive caffeine, and even the timing of your meals can all contribute to elevated cortisol levels.

The Science Behind Cortisol and Diet

Your cortisol level can be helped to be regulated by food. All of which help to create a healthier stress response, the correct nutrients can soothe your nervous system, nourish your adrenal glands, and even encourage better sleep.

Although there is no one-size-fits-all diet for cortisol balance, several foods and eating habits can either fight or fuel elevated cortisol.

Foods That Increase Cortisol:

🚫 Highly processed foods (think sugary snacks, fast food, and refined carbs)
🚫 Excess caffeine (too much coffee can send your cortisol skyrocketing)
🚫 Alcohol (disrupts sleep and increases stress on the liver)
🚫 Skipping meals (causes blood sugar crashes, which trigger cortisol release)

Foods That Help Lower Cortisol:

☑ Healthy fats (avocados, ghee, nuts, seeds, and olive oil help regulate hormones)
☑ Protein-rich foods (help stabilize blood sugar and prevent energy crashes)
☑ Magnesium-rich foods (dark chocolate, leafy greens, nuts—nature's stress relievers)
☑ Herbal teas and adaptogens (chamomile, ashwagandha, and mint can calm your system)

By making **small, intentional changes** to the way you eat, you can naturally support your body in reducing stress and feeling more balanced.

ⓐ Eat at Regular Intervals: Why Skipping Meals Spikes Cortisol

Did you know that **skipping meals can actually make your stress levels worse?**

When you go too long without eating, your blood sugar drops. Your body sees this as an emergency and **releases cortisol to bring blood sugar back up**—causing more stress.

Signs that erratic eating is raising your cortisol:
- ✔ Feeling jittery, lightheaded, or irritable between meals
- ✔ Crashing in the afternoon and needing caffeine or sugar to keep going
- ✔ Waking up in the middle of the night feeling anxious or hungry

How to fix it:
- ☑ **Eat every 3-4 hours** to prevent blood sugar crashes.
- ☑ **Prioritize protein + healthy fats at every meal** for sustained energy.
- ☑ **Don't fear carbs—just choose the right ones!** Whole grains, sweet potatoes, and quinoa help keep blood sugar stable.

By **fueling your body consistently**, you're signaling to your brain that you are **safe, nourished, and not in survival mode**—which helps **keep cortisol levels in check.**

The Role of Lifestyle and Nutrition in Balancing Stress Hormones

Cortisol is not just about stress. It's a finely tuned system that responds to **everything** you do—your diet, sleep patterns, exercise routine, emotional state, and even the way you breathe.

See your body as a little ecosystem. Your body requires the proper mix of food, exercise, rest, and emotional control to control cortisol, much as a rainforest depends on the proper balance of sunlight, water, and nutrition to survive.
Should one of these components—say, poor sleep, overworking, or skipping meals—be off, your cortisol levels will react. This imbalance can cascade over time and cause weight gain, chronic tiredness, mood changes, and a compromised immune system.

So, what can you do to bring things back into balance? Let's break it down step by step.

🌙 Prioritize Sleep: The Ultimate Cortisol Reset

If there's one lifestyle habit that makes a **huge** impact on cortisol, it's sleep. Sleep is like a reset button for your nervous system. When you **don't get enough** of it, your body perceives this as stress—raising cortisol levels to keep you alert.

The science behind sleep and cortisol:

- **Cortisol follows a natural rhythm**—it should be highest in the morning to wake you up and lowest at night to allow deep sleep.

- Poor sleep causes **cortisol to stay high at night**, making it harder to fall asleep and creating a vicious cycle of stress and exhaustion.

- Lack of sleep **impairs insulin sensitivity**, making blood sugar spikes and cravings worse the next day.

Signs that high cortisol is disrupting your sleep:

✔ Waking up in the middle of the night and struggling to fall back asleep
✔ Feeling *tired but wired* at bedtime—exhausted but unable to relax
✔ Having intense sugar or carb cravings at night
✔ Feeling groggy and unfocused even after a full night's rest

How to fix it:

☑ **Stick to a consistent bedtime:** Going to sleep at the same time every night helps regulate your body's internal clock.

☑ **Limit blue light exposure:** The light from phones, TVs, and computers tricks your brain into thinking it's still daytime. Try dimming the lights an hour before bed.

☑ **Eat a light, cortisol-friendly dinner:** Avoid heavy, high-sugar meals before bed. Opt for **a protein-rich dinner with healthy fats and slow-digesting carbs** to keep blood sugar stable.

☑ **Try magnesium or herbal tea:** Magnesium-rich foods (like dark chocolate, almonds, and leafy greens) or a cup of chamomile tea can work wonders.

The goal? **Create an evening ritual that tells your body, "Hey, it's time to relax."**

🚶 Why More Exercise Isn't Always Better? Move Your Body (the Right Way).

Most people believe that greater health results from more exercise. Regarding cortisol, though, the kind of activity you undertake counts more than its quantity.

The link between cortisol-exercise:

- If done too often, intense workouts—including HIIT, jogging, or too much cardio—can actually raise cortisol.
- Overtraining without enough recuperation keeps your body in a continual fight-or-flight mode, which causes muscle loss, inflammation, and tiredness.
- Gentle movement—walking, yoga, stretching—tells your body it is safe to relax, therefore naturally reducing cortisol levels.

Signs you may be over-exercising and increasing cortisol:

✔ Constant fatigue and lack of motivation

✔ Difficulty losing weight despite intense workouts

✔ Increased sugar cravings and mid-day energy crashes

✔ Feeling drained rather than energized after exercise

How to fix it:

☑ **Incorporate gentle movement**—walking, swimming, pilates, or yin yoga are amazing for lowering cortisol.

☑ **Give strength training top priority** over too much cardio; resistance training balances hormones without adding to stress load.

☑ **Listen to your body**— if you feel tired, schedule a rest day! More does not always mean better.

Your body runs on movement, but it shouldn't feel like punishment. The aim is to live in a way that supports rather than opposes your hormones.

Practice Deep Breathing & Mindfulness: Your Fastest Path to Lower Cortisol

Here's something wild—**your breath is directly connected to your cortisol levels.**

When you're **stressed, overwhelmed, or anxious**, your breathing becomes **shallow and rapid**. This tells your body, *we're in danger*, which **triggers even more cortisol production.**

But when you slow down your breath, you send the opposite message: "We're safe."

How deep breathing lowers cortisol:

- Activates the **parasympathetic nervous system (rest and digest mode)**
- Lowers heart rate and blood pressure
- Reduces inflammation and improves digestion

Try this right now:
Box Breathing (4-4-4-4 Method)

1. Inhale through your nose for **4 seconds**
2. Hold your breath for **4 seconds**
3. Exhale slowly through your mouth for **4 seconds**
4. Hold your breath for **4 seconds**, then repeat

J

ust **2 minutes** of deep breathing can **reduce cortisol levels almost instantly.**

Other great cortisol-lowering mindfulness practices:
☑ **Journaling**—writing down your thoughts helps process emotions and clear mental clutter.
☑ **Gratitude practice**—focusing on what you're grateful for shifts your brain away from stress mode.
☑ **Grounding exercises**—walking barefoot in nature or sitting in sunlight helps reset your nervous system.

These small, simple shifts can make **a profound difference** in how you feel every day.

Bringing It All Together: A Lifestyle That Supports Low Cortisol

Managing cortisol isn't about making drastic changes overnight. It's about **making small, sustainable shifts** that allow your body to **feel safe, nourished, and supported.**

When you **combine a balanced diet with restorative lifestyle habits**, you're not just lowering cortisol—you're **building a foundation for long-term health.**

✔ Prioritize **quality sleep**
✔ Choose **exercise that supports your body, not depletes it**
✔ Practice **deep breathing and mindfulness** daily
✔ **Eat regularly** to keep blood sugar stable

Every little change adds up. And over time? **You'll feel the difference—calmer, more energized, and in control of your health.**

Key Nutrients for a Cortisol-Balancing Diet

Balancing cortisol isn't about following a **rigid diet** or **eliminating entire food groups**. It's about **nourishing your body with the right nutrients**—the ones that help stabilize blood sugar, support adrenal health, and reduce inflammation.

Think of it this way: **Your body is like a well-oiled machine.** Every system, from your brain to your digestion, needs the **right fuel** to function properly. And when cortisol is out of balance, it's often a sign that your body is running on **the wrong kind of fuel**—too much sugar, too little protein, not enough healthy fats, and a lack of key vitamins and minerals.

This chapter is about **getting back to the basics**—the foundational nutrients your body needs to **naturally regulate stress hormones and keep cortisol in check.**

Protein and Healthy Fats: The Cornerstones of Hormonal Balance

If you're constantly dealing with **mood swings, energy crashes, or sugar cravings**, chances are your **protein and healthy fat intake** needs some adjusting.

Why Protein Is Essential for Cortisol Regulation

Protein isn't just for building muscle—it's essential for **hormonal balance, stable blood sugar, and adrenal function.**

When you don't eat enough protein, your blood sugar levels fluctuate **more dramatically**, triggering **cortisol spikes** to compensate. Protein helps **slow down the absorption of sugar into your bloodstream**, preventing those energy crashes that send you running for caffeine or sweets.

How protein supports cortisol balance:
- ✔ Provides **amino acids** that are essential for neurotransmitter production (think serotonin for calmness and dopamine for motivation)
- ✔ **Stabilizes blood sugar** and prevents stress-induced sugar cravings
- ✔ Supports **adrenal gland function**—your adrenals need protein to produce the right balance of hormones

Best cortisol-friendly protein sources:

- ☑ **Wild-caught fish** – High in omega-3s, which reduce inflammation
- ☑ **Pasture-raised eggs** – Rich in choline, essential for brain and nerve function
- ☑ **Grass-fed beef and poultry** – Full of B vitamins that support adrenal health
- ☑ **Bone broth and collagen** – Gut-healing and packed with amino acids
- ☑ **Plant-based proteins (lentils, quinoa, hemp seeds)** – Great for variety and fiber intake

Pro tip: Start your day with protein! A protein-rich breakfast (like eggs with avocado or a smoothie with collagen, bone broth etc) helps **set the stage for balanced blood sugar and lower cortisol all day.**

The Power of Healthy Fats for Hormonal Balance

For decades, **fats were demonized**, but the truth is, **your hormones depend on them.** Every single hormone in your body—including cortisol—is built from cholesterol and fats. Without enough healthy fats, **your body struggles to produce and regulate hormones properly.**

How healthy fats support cortisol balance:

- ✔ **Reduce inflammation**, preventing cortisol from staying elevated
- ✔ **Support brain function**, reducing brain fog and stress-related anxiety
- ✔ **Slow digestion**, keeping blood sugar stable and preventing spikes

Best cortisol-friendly fats:

- ☑ **Avocados** – Rich in fiber and monounsaturated fats. Good anytime of the day.
- ☑ **Coconut oil** – Provides quick, clean-burning energy for adrenal function
- ☑ **Extra virgin olive oil** – Anti-inflammatory and heart-healthy
- ☑ **Fatty fish (salmon, mackerel, sardines)** – High in omega-3s, which lower stress hormones
- ☑ **Nuts & seeds (walnuts, almond, flaxseeds, chia seeds)** – Great sources of magnesium and essential fatty acids

Pro tip: Pairing protein with healthy fats (like salmon with avocado or nuts with Greek yogurt) helps **keep you full longer and prevents cortisol-triggering blood sugar crashes.**

The Impact of Carbohydrates on Stress and Energy Levels

Carbs often get a **bad reputation**, but **they are NOT the enemy**—especially when it comes to **balancing cortisol**.

Carbohydrates play a **critical role** in helping your body regulate stress hormones. But **not all carbs are created equal**—some **stabilize** cortisol, while others **trigger** it.

Why Low-Carb Diets Can Backfire for High Cortisol

If you've ever tried a **low-carb or keto** diet and felt **exhausted, irritable, or couldn't sleep well**, it's because **your body needs a certain amount of carbs to regulate cortisol**.

Carbohydrates **help bring cortisol levels down**, especially in the evening. That's why people on **very low-carb diets** often experience **sleep disturbances and increased anxiety**—their cortisol isn't dropping the way it should.

Best cortisol-friendly carbohydrates:
- ☑ **Sweet potatoes** – Slow-digesting and packed with vitamins
- ☑ **Quinoa** – A great plant-based protein-carb hybrid
- ☑ **Oats** – Full of fiber and calming for the nervous system
- ☑ **Brown rice** – A steady, slow-burning source of energy
- ☑ **Berries & apples** – Low in sugar but high in fiber and antioxidants

Micronutrients That Support Adrenal Health

Beyond macronutrients, your adrenal glands need **specific vitamins and minerals** to function properly.

Key Nutrients for Lowering Cortisol

- ◆ **Magnesium** – Best mineral for relaxation and that **reduces stress and promotes sleep**
Found in: Dark chocolate, spinach, almonds, pumpkin seeds

- ◆ **Vitamin C** – Supports **adrenal function and fights inflammation**
Found in: Bell peppers, oranges, strawberries, kiwi

- ◆ **B Vitamins** – Very essential vitamin for **energy production and nervous system health.**
(Especially for vegans and vegetarians)
Found in: Leafy greens, eggs, meat, whole grains

- ◆ **Zinc** – Is great at helping to regulate the **HPA axis**, which controls cortisol release
Found in: Pumpkin seeds, lentils, beef, chickpeas

- ◆ **Omega-3 Fatty Acids – Are the best for reducing inflammation and supporting brain function**
Found in: Salmon, walnuts, flaxseeds, chia seeds

If you're feeling **burnt out or constantly stressed**, chances are you may be deficient in **one or more of these key nutrients**.

Pro tip: Focus on nutrient-dense, whole foods rather than relying on supplements.

The Role of Gut Health in Cortisol Regulation

Did you know that **over 90% of serotonin (your happy, calming neurotransmitter) is produced in the gut**? That means if your gut is inflamed or unhealthy, **your stress levels will be higher, and cortisol will be harder to regulate.** It is very important to have in mind that your food is also food for your gut microbiome and bacteria.

How gut health impacts cortisol:
- ✔ A balanced gut microbiome **reduces inflammation and stress hormones**
- ✔ Healthy digestion **ensures proper absorption of cortisol-lowering nutrients**
- ✔ A strong gut lining **prevents toxins from triggering an immune-stress response**

Best gut-healing foods for cortisol balance:
- ☑ **Fermented foods (kimchi, sauerkraut, kefir, yogurt)** – Strengthen the gut microbiome, gives it the good kind of bacteria.
- ☑ **Bone broth** – Rich in collagen to support the gut lining. Goof to drink In the morning on empty stomach.
- ☑ **Prebiotic fibers (onions, garlic, asparagus, bananas)** – Feed beneficial gut bacteria

Final Thoughts: Your Personalized Blueprint for Cortisol Balance

By **incorporating these key nutrients into your daily diet**, you're not just **eating healthier,** you're **reprogramming your body to handle stress better, stabilize energy, and feel more balanced.**

The golden formula for cortisol balance:

- ✓ **Protein + Healthy Fats** at every meal

- ✓ **Complex Carbs in the evening** for better sleep

- ✓ **Plenty of Magnesium, Vitamin C, and B Vitamins**

- ✓ **A focus on gut health to support stress resilience**

When you **nourish your body with what it truly needs, your cortisol levels naturally start to regulate**—and you start feeling like *your best self again.*

Breakfast Recipes

Yoghurt & Berries Bowl

Servings|2   Time|10 minutes
Nutritional Content (per serving):
Cal| 167   Fat|3.4g   Protein| 7g   Carbs|29.5g   Fibre|4.6g

Ingredients:

- 250 g (1 C.) reduced-fat plain Greek yoghurt
- ¾ g (¼ tsp.) powdered cinnamon
- 25 g (¼ C.) unsalted almonds, cut up
- 40 g (2 tbsp.) raw honey
- 280 g (2 C.) fresh mixed berries

Directions:

1. Into a basin Put the yoghurt, sugar and cinnamon and blend to incorporate.
2. Divide yoghurt into serving dishes.
3. Top with berries and almonds and enjoy right away.

Fruity Green Smoothie Bowl

Servings|2   Time|10 minutes
Nutritional Content (per serving):
Cal| 225   Fat| 7.2g   Protein| 4.9g   Carbs| 40.2g   Fibre| 8g

Ingredients:

- 125 g (1 C.) fresh strawberries, hulled
- ¼ of ripe avocado, peeled, pitted & cut up
- 55 g (1 C.) fresh baby kale
- 360 ml (1½ C.) unsweetened almond milk
- 2 frozen bananas, peeled & sliced
- 30 g (1 C.) fresh spinach
- 10 g (1 tbsp.) flaxseed meal

Directions:

1. Put the strawberries and remnant ingredients into an electric blender and process to form a smooth mixture.
2. Enjoy right away with your favorite topping.

Overnight Oatmeal

Servings|2   Time|10 minutes
Nutritional Content (per serving):
Cal| 203   Fat| 4.4g   Protein| 5.7g   Carbs| 36.2g   Fibre| 6g

Ingredients:

- 100 g (1 C.) gluten-free rolled oats
- 10 g (2 tsp.) raw honey
- 40 g (¼ C.) fresh blueberries
- 1¼ g (½ tsp.) powdered cinnamon
- 240 ml (1 C.) unsweetened almond milk

Directions:

1. Put the oats and remnant ingredients except for blueberries into a large-sized basin and blend to incorporate thoroughly.
2. Cover the basin and put into your fridge overnight.
3. In the morning, top with blueberries and enjoy.

Flaxseed Meal Porridge

Servings|4   Time|18 minutes
Nutritional Content (per serving):
Cal| 243   Fat| 16g   Protein| 2.2g   Carbs| 20.9g   Fibre| 6.7g

Ingredients:

- 2 ripe bananas, peeled & mashed
- 40 g (¼ C.) flaxseed meal
- 1¼ g (½ tsp.) powdered cinnamon
- Pinch of sea salt
- 75 g (¾ C.) almond meal
- 1¼ g (½ tsp.) powdered ginger
- ¼ g (1/8 tsp.) powdered nutmeg
- 480 ml (2 C.) unsweetened almond milk

Directions:

1. Put the bananas and remnant ingredients into a medium-sized, heavy-bottomed pot and blend to incorporate.
2. Put the pot of banana mixture on burner at around medium-low heat.
3. Cook the mixture until boiling, mixing all the time.
4. Cook for around 2-3 minutes, mixing all the time.
5. Enjoy with your desired topping.

Overnight Seeds Porridge

Servings|2   Time|10 minutes
Nutritional Content (per serving):
Cal| 392   Fat| 28.1g   Protein| 14.7g   Carbs| 10g   Fibre| 5.7g

Ingredients:

- 210 ml ((¾ C.) plus 2 tbsp.) unsweetened almond milk, divided
- 20 g (1 tbsp.) raw honey
- Pinch of sea salt
- 80 g (½ C.) hemp hearts
- 20 g (1 tbsp.) chia seeds
- 2½ ml (½ tsp.) organic vanilla extract
- 20 g (2 tbsp.) pumpkin seeds

Directions:

1. Put 210 ml of almond milk, hemp hearts, chia seed, honey, vanilla extract and salt into a large-sized airtight container and blend to incorporate thoroughly.
2. Cover the container tightly and put into your fridge overnight.
3. Just before enjoying Put the in remnant almond milk and blend to incorporate.
4. Add fruit if you want some additional sweetness and vitamins.
5. Enjoy right away.

Nuts, Seeds & Chia Porridge

Servings|5 Time|45 minutes
Nutritional Content (per serving):
Cal| 282   Fat| 25.1g   Protein| 7.4g   Carbs| 12.2g   Fibre| 5.7g

Ingredients:
- 65 g (½ C.) unsalted pecans
- 25 g (¼ C.) unsalted almonds
- 40 g (¼ C.) chia seeds
- 1¼ g (½ tsp.) powdered cinnamon
- 50 g (½ C.) unsalted walnuts
- 35 g (¼ C.) sunflower seeds
- 960 ml (4 C.) unsweetened almond milk
- 20 g (1 tbsp.) raw honey

Directions:
1. Put the pecans, walnuts, almonds and sunflower seeds into an electric food processor and process to form a crumbly mixture.
2. Put the nut mixture, chia seeds, almond milk, spices and honey into a large-sized pot on burner at around medium heat.
3. Cook the mixture until boiling, stirring frequently. Turn the heat at around low.
4. Cook for around 20-30 minutes, stirring frequently. Take off the pot of porridge from burner and enjoy right away.

Quinoa Porridge

Servings|4 Time|30 minutes
Nutritional Content (per serving):
Cal| 249   Fat| 7.1g   Protein| 8.7g   Carbs| 36.2g   Fibre| 5.7g

Ingredients:
- 190 g (1 C.) quinoa, rinsed
- 5 ml (1 tsp.) organic vanilla extract
- 40 g (2 tbsp.) pure maple syrup
- 40 g (¼ C.) fresh blueberries
- 360 ml (1½ C.) unsweetened almond milk
- 2½ g (1 tsp.) powdered cinnamon
- 30 g (2 tbsp.) peanut butter

Directions:
1. Put the quinoa, almond milk, vanilla extract and cinnamon into a medium-sized pot on burner at around medium heat. Cook the mixture until boiling.
2. Turn the heat at around low. Cook with the cover for around 15 minutes.
3. Take off the pot of quinoa from burner and blend in maple syrup and peanut butter.
4. Enjoy moderately hot with the topping of berries.

Oats & Buckwheat Granola

Servings|12   Time|1 hour
Nutritional Content (per serving):
Cal| 312   Fat| 15.1g   Protein| 8.3g   Carbs| 39.2g   Fibre| 6.7g

Ingredients:

- ❖ Olive oil baking spray
- ❖ 130 g (1 C.) pumpkin seeds
- ❖ 170 g (1 C.) buckwheat
- ❖ 225 g (1 C.) fresh apple puree
- ❖ 5 g (1 tbsp.) fresh ginger root, finely grated

- ❖ 200 g (2 C.) gluten-free oats
- ❖ 140 g (1 C.) sunflower seeds
- ❖ 225 g (1½ C.) dates, pitted & cut up
- ❖ 90 g (1/3 C.) almond butter
- ❖ 30 g (¼ C.) cacao powder

Directions:

1. For preheating: set your oven at 175 °C (350 °F).
2. Spray a large-sized baking pan with baking spray.
3. Put the oats, seeds and buckwheat into a basin and blend to incorporate.
4. Put the dates, apple puree and almond butter into a small-sized pot and blend to incorporate.
5. Put the pot on burner at around medium-low heat.
6. Cook for around 5 minutes, stirring frequently.
7. Blend in ginger and take off from burner.
8. Set aside to cool slightly.
9. Put the date mixture and cacao powder into an electric blender and process to form a smooth mixture.
10. Put the date mixture in the basin with oat mixture and blend to incorporate well
11. Put the oat mixture into the baking pan and spread in an even layer.
12. Bake for around 15 minutes.
13. Take off the baking pan of granola from oven and blend thoroughly.
14. Bake for around 30 minutes, stirring after every 5-10 minutes.
15. This granola can be preserved into an airtight container.

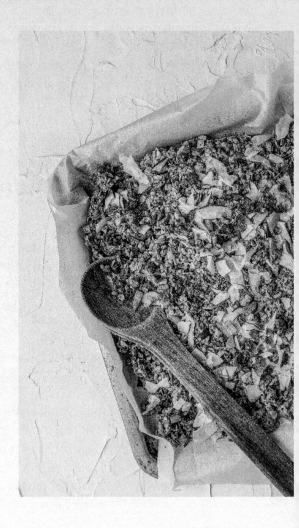

Blueberry Waffles

Servings|5 Time|35 minutes
Nutritional Content (per serving):
Cal| 280   Fat| 23.1g   Protein| 12.2g   Carbs| 8.2g   Fibre| 5.1g

Ingredients:

- 1 large egg (white & yolk separated)
- 5 g (1¼ tsp.) baking powder
- 60 ml (¼ C.) unsweetened almond milk
- 2½ ml (½ tsp.) organic vanilla extract
- 125 g (1¼ C.) almond flour
- Pinch of sea salt
- 20 g (1 tbsp.) pure maple syrup
- Olive oil baking spray

Directions:

1. Put the egg white into a medium-sized basin and with a hand-held electric beater, whisk on high speed to form soft peaks.
2. Put the egg yolk and remnant ingredients into a large-sized basin and with a hand-held electric beater, whisk on high speed to incorporate thoroughly.
3. Lightly blend in whipped egg white.
4. Preheat your waffle iron and then grease it with baking spray.
5. Place desired amount of mixture into preheated waffle iron.
6. Cook for around 5 minutes.
7. Cook the remnant waffles in the very same method and add blueberries on top.

Vanilla Pancakes

Servings|5 Time|30 minutes
Nutritional Content (per serving):
Cal| 276   Fat| 14.1g   Protein| 4.7g   Carbs| 32.2g   Fibre| 4.8g

Ingredients:

- ❖ 240 ml (1 C.) unsweetened almond milk
- ❖ 125 g (1 C.) buckwheat flour
- ❖ 12 g (1 tbsp.) baking powder
- ❖ 75 g (¼ C.) pure maple syrup
- ❖ 15-30 ml (1-2 tbsp.) olive oil

- ❖ 10 ml (2 tsp.) apple cider vinegar
- ❖ 20 g (2 tbsp.) flaxseed meal
- ❖ Pinch of sea salt
- ❖ 5 ml (1 tsp.) organic vanilla extract

Directions:

1. Put the almond milk and vinegar into a medium-sized basin and blend to incorporate. Set aside.
2. Put the flour, flax seed, baking powder and salt into a large-sized basin and blend to incorporate.
3. Put the almond milk mixture, maple syrup and vanilla extract and whisk to incorporate thoroughly.
4. Sizzle oil into a large-sized anti-sticking wok on burner at around medium heat.
5. Place desired amount of mixture and spread in an even circle.
6. Cook for around 2 minutes.
7. Flip and cook for around 1-2 minutes.
8. Cook the remnant pancakes in the very same method.
9. Enjoy moderately hot.

Blueberry Muffins

Servings|12   Time|40 minutes
Nutritional Content (per serving):
Cal| 252   Fat| 18.1g   Protein| 1.4g   Carbs| 14.2g   Fibre| 4.4g

Ingredients:

- ❖ Olive oil baking spray
- ❖ 5 g (1 tbsp.) coconut flour
- ❖ 7½ g (3 tsp.) powdered cinnamon, divided
- ❖ 2 eggs
- ❖ 60 ml (¼ C.) olive oil
- ❖ 5 ml (1 tsp.) organic vanilla extract

- ❖ 250 g (2½ C.) almond flour
- ❖ 2 g (½ tsp.) baking soda
- ❖ Pinch of sea salt
- ❖ 60 ml (¼ C.) unsweetened almond milk
- ❖ 75 g (¼ C.) raw honey
- ❖ 150 g (1 C.) fresh blueberries

Directions:

1. For preheating: set your oven at 175 °C (350 °F).
2. Spray a 12 holes muffin tin with baking spray.
3. Put the flours, baking soda, half of cinnamon and salt into a large-sized basin and blend to incorporate.
4. Put the eggs, milk, oil, honey and vanilla extract into another medium-sized basin and whisk to incorporate thoroughly.
5. Put the egg mixture in the basin of flour mixture and blend to incorporate thoroughly.
6. Lightly blend in blueberries.
7. Put the mixture into the muffin C. and sprinkle each with cinnamon.
8. Bake for around 22-25 minutes.
9. Take off the muffin tin from oven and place onto a cooling metal rack to cool for around 10 minutes.
10. Then invert the muffins onto the metal rack to cool thoroughly before enjoying.

Carrot Bread

Servings|8   Time|1¼ hours
Nutritional Content (per serving):
Cal| 240   Fat| 19.1g   Protein| 8.7g   Carbs| 12.2g   Fibre| 5.7g

Ingredients:

- ❖ 200 g (2 C.) almond meal
- ❖ 1¼ g (½ tsp.) powdered cinnamon
- ❖ 3 eggs
- ❖ 30 ml (2 tbsp.) olive oil
- ❖ 225 g (2½ C.) carrots, peeled & grated
- ❖ 30 g (¼ C.) unsalted walnuts, cut up

- ❖ 4 g (1 tsp.) baking powder
- ❖ Pinch of sea salt
- ❖ 75 g (¼ C.) raw honey
- ❖ 15 ml (1 tbsp.) apple cider vinegar
- ❖ 5 g (1 tbsp.) fresh ginger root, grated

Directions:

1. For preheating: set your oven at 175 °C (350 °F).
2. Lay out bakery paper into a loaf pan.
3. Put the almond meal, baking powder, cinnamon and salt into a large-sized basin and blend to incorporate.
4. Put the eggs, honey, oil and vinegar into another basin and whisk to incorporate thoroughly.
5. Put the egg mixture into the flour mixture and blend to incorporate thoroughly.
6. Lightly blend in carrot, ginger and walnuts.
7. Pace the mixture into the loaf pan.
8. Bake for around 1 hour.
9. Take off the loaf pan from your oven and Put the onto a counter to cool for at least 12-15 minutes.
10. Take off the bread from pan and lay out onto a platter to cool thoroughly before enjoying.

Salmon & Spinach Scramble

Servings|2   Time|20 minutes
Nutritional Content (per serving):
Cal| 239   Fat| 16.1g   Protein| 19.7g   Carbs| 1.9g   Fibre| 0.2g

Ingredients:

- 60 g (2 C.) fresh spinach, finely cut up
- Pinch of sea salt
- 140 g (5 oz.) cooked unsalted unsalted salmon, finely cut up
- 15 ml (1 tbsp.) olive oil
- Powdered black pepper, as desired
- 4 eggs, whisked

Directions:

1. Sizzle oil into a wok on burner at around high heat.
2. Cook the spinach with salt and pepper for around 1-2 minutes.
3. Blend in salmon and turn the heat around medium.
4. Put in eggs and cook for around 3-4 minutes, stirring frequently.

Apple Omelet

Servings|2   Time|20 minutes
Nutritional Content (per serving):
Cal| 206   Fat| 15.1g   Protein| 12.7g   Carbs| 0.8g   Fibre| 0.2g

Ingredients:

- 15 ml (3 tsp.) olive oil, divided
- ¾ g (¼ tsp.) powdered cinnamon
- ¾ g (¼ tsp.) powdered nutmeg
- 1¼ ml (¼ tsp.) organic vanilla extract
- 1 large green apple, cored & and thinly sliced
- 4 large eggs
- Pinch of sea salt

Directions:

1. Sizzle half of oil into an anti-sticking frying pan on burner at around medium-low heat.
2. Cook the apple slices with nutmeg and cinnamon for around 4-5 minutes, flipping once halfway through.
3. In the meantime, Put the eggs, vanilla extract and salt into a basin and whisk until fluffy.
4. Put the remnant oil into the frying pan and let it sizzle thoroughly.
5. Put the egg mixture over apple slices and cook for around 3-4 minutes.
6. Carefully turn the pot over a serving plate and immediately fold the omelet.
7. Cut the omelet into 2 portions and enjoy right away.

Veggies Frittata

Servings|3   Time|30 minutes
Nutritional Content (per serving):
Cal| 191   Fat| 12.1g   Protein| 12.4g   Carbs| 6.4g   Fibre| 1.2g

Ingredients:

- 15 ml (1 tbsp.) olive oil
- 1 medium capsicum, seeded & cut up
- 50 g (¼ C.) green onion, cut up
- 6 eggs
- Powdered black pepper, as desired
- 1¼ g (½ tsp.) powdered turmeric
- 55 g (1 C.) fresh kale leaves, tough ribs removed & cut up
- Pinch of sea salt

Directions:

1. Sizzle oil into a cast-iron wok on burner at around medium-low heat.
2. Sprinkle turmeric in the oil and immediately blend in capsicum, kale and green onion greens.
3. Cook for around 2 minutes, stirring all the time.
4. In the meantime, Put the eggs, salt and pepper into a basin and whisk thoroughly.
5. Turn the heat at around low.
6. Put the whisked eggs in the wok over capsicum mixture.
7. Cover and cook for around 10-15 minutes.
8. Take off the wok of frittata from burner and set aside for around 5 minutes before enjoying.
9. Cut into serving portions and enjoy.

Lunch Recipes

Citrus Greens Salad

Servings|2   Time|10 minutes
Nutritional Content (per serving):
Cal| 256   Fat| 13.2g   Protein| 4.8g   Carbs| 31.2g   Fibre| 4.9g

Ingredients:

- 30 g (1 C.) fresh baby spinach
- 25 g (1 C.) fresh baby arugula
- 1 grapefruit, peeled & segmented
- 30 ml (2 tbsp.) olive oil
- 5 g (1 tsp.) Dijon mustard
- Pinch of sea salt

- 55 g (1 C.) fresh baby kale
- 1 orange, peeled & segmented
- 15 g (2 tbsp.) fresh cranberries
- 30 ml (2 tbsp.) fresh orange juice
- 2½ g (½ tsp.) raw honey
- Powdered black pepper, as desired

Directions:

1. For the salad: put the greens, orange, grapefruit and cranberries into a salad dish and blend.
2. For the dressing: put the oil, orange juice, mustard, honey, salt and pepper into another basin and whisk to incorporate thoroughly.
3. Place dressing on top of salad and toss to incorporate thoroughly.
4. Enjoy right away.

Egg & Avocado Salad

Servings|4   Time|15 minutes
Nutritional Content (per serving):
Cal| 240   Fat| 16.1g   Protein| 7g   Carbs| 6g   Fibre| 3.2g

Ingredients:

- 30 ml (2 tbsp.) olive oil
- Pinch of sea salt
- 120 g (4 C.) fresh baby spinach
- 2 medium avocados, peeled, pitted & sliced

- 30 ml (2 tbsp.) fresh lime juice
- Powdered black pepper, as desired
- 4 hard-boiled eggs, peeled & sliced
- 2½ g (1 tbsp.) fresh mint leaves

Directions:

1. For the dressing: put the oil, lime juice, salt and pepper into a small-sized basin and whisk to incorporate thoroughly.
2. Put the greens onto a serving plate and top with egg, avocado slices and mint.
3. Drizzle with dressing and enjoy.

Bulgur Salad

Servings|4   Time|15 minutes
Nutritional Content (per serving):
Cal| 226   Fat| 11.1g   Protein| 8.7g   Carbs| 26.2g   Fibre| 8.7g

Ingredients:

- 95 g (½ C.) uncooked bulgur
- 3 medium tomatoes, cut up
- 10 g (½ C.) fresh mint, cut up
-
- 30 ml (2 tbsp.) olive oil
- Pinch of sea salt

- 480 ml (2 C.) hot salt-free vegetable broth
- 10 g (½ C.) fresh parsley, cut up
- 25 g (¼ C.) green onions, cut up
- 30 ml (2 tbsp.) fresh lemon juice

Directions:

1. Put the bulgur and broth into a large-sized basin and set aside with a cover for around 30-60 minutes.
2. Through a fine-mesh strainer, strain the bulgur and transfer into a large-sized serving dish.
3. Put the in the remnant ingredients in the dish of bulgur and blend to incorporate thoroughly.
4. Enjoy right away.

Chickpea Lettuce Wraps

Servings|4   Time|40 minutes
Nutritional Content (per serving):
Cal| 318   Fat| 18.1g   Protein| 7.5g   Carbs| 34.2g   Fibre| 9.7g

Ingredients:

- 1 (16-oz.) can no-salt-added chickpeas, rinsed, drained and pat dried
- ¾ g (¼ tsp.) powdered cumin
- 1 avocado, peeled, pitted & cut up
- 30 ml (2 tbsp.) olive oil
- ¾ g (¼ tsp.) paprika
- 8 large lettuce leaves
- 300 g (2 C.) cherry tomatoes, halved

Directions:

1. For preheating: set your oven at 205 °C (400 °F).
2. Lay out bakery paper onto a large-sized baking tray.
3. Put the chickpeas, oil, spices and salt into a basin and toss to incorporate thoroughly.
4. Arrange the chickpeas onto the baking tray. Bake for around 20-25 minutes.
5. Transfer the chickpeas into a glass basin and set aside to cool.
6. Arrange the lettuce leaves onto serving plates. Divide the chickpeas, avocado and tomatoes over each leaf.

Chicken Stuffed Avocado

Servings|2   Time|15 minutes
Nutritional Content (per serving):
Cal| 282   Fat| 15.4g   Protein| 23.7g   Carbs| 9.9g   Fibre| 5.2g

Ingredients:

- 140 g (1 C.) cooked unsalted chicken, shredded
- 30 g (¼ C.) onion, finely cut up
- 5 g (1 tsp.) Dijon mustard
- Pinch of cayenne pepper powder
- Powdered black pepper, as desired
- 1 avocado, halved and pitted
- 15 ml (1 tbsp.) fresh lime juice
- 65 g (¼ C.) reduced-fat plain Greek yoghurt
- Pinch of sea salt

Directions:

1. With a scooper, scoop out the flesh from the middle of each avocado half and transfer into a basin.
2. Put the lime juice and mash to incorporate thoroughly.
3. Put the remnant ingredients and blend to incorporate.
4. Divide the chicken mixture into avocado halves and enjoy it right away.

Tuna Sandwiches

Servings|2　Time|10 minutes
Nutritional Content (per serving):
Cal| 283　Fat| 4g　Protein| 25.7g　Carbs| 40.2g　Fibre| 6.2g

Ingredients:
- 1 (140-g) (5-oz.) can water-packed tuna, drained
- 5 g (1 tsp.) mustard
- 2½ g (½ tsp.) raw honey
- 2 lettuce leaves
- 1 medium apple, peeled, cored & cut up
- 45 g (3 tbsp.) reduced-fat plain Greek yoghurt
- 4 whole-meal bread slices

Directions:
1. Put the tuna, apple, yoghurt mustard and honey into a basin and blend to incorporate thoroughly.
2. Spread the tuna mix over each of 2 bread slices.
3. Top each sandwich with 1 lettuce leaf.
4. Close with the remnant bread slices.
5. Cut the sandwiches in half and enjoy.

Turkey Koftas

Servings|6　Time|25 minutes
Nutritional Content (per serving):
Cal| 178　Fat| 7.3g　Protein| 23.7g　Carbs| 3g　Fibre| 0.9g

Ingredients:
- 455 g (1 lb.) extra-lean ground turkey
- 15 g (2 tbsp.) onion, grated
- 2 garlic cloves, minced
- 2½ g (1 tsp.) powdered coriander
- 2½ g (1 tsp.) powdered turmeric
- Powdered black pepper, as desired
- 300 g (6 C.) romaine lettuce, torn
- 30 g (2 tbsp.) reduced-fat plain Greek yoghurt
- 2½ g (2 tbsp.) fresh coriander, finely cut up
- 2½ g (1 tsp.) powdered cumin
- Pinch of sea salt
- 30 ml (2 tbsp.) olive oil

Directions:
1. For koftas: put the ground turkey and remnant ingredients except for oil and lettuce into a large-sized basin and blend to incorporate thoroughly. Shape the mixture into 12 oblong shaped patties.
2. Sizzle oil into a large-sized anti-sticking wok on burner at around medium-high heat.
3. Cook the patties for around 10 minutes, flipping time to time.
4. Divide the lettuce and koftas onto serving plates.

Salmon Burgers

Servings|5   Time|25 minutes
Nutritional Content (per serving):
Cal| 280   Fat| 12.1g   Protein| 22.7g   Carbs| 17.2g   Fibre| 2.7g

Ingredients:

- 5 ml (1 tsp.) olive oil
- 45 g (1/3 C.) shallots, finely cut up
- Pinch of sea salt
- 455 g (1 lb.) skinless salmon fillets
- 40 g (2 tbsp.) Dijon mustard
- 1¼ g (½ tsp.) powdered cumin
- Olive oil baking spray

- 55 g (1 C.) fresh kale, tough ribs removed & cut up
- Powdered black pepper, as desired
- 140 g (¾ C.) cooked unsalted quinoa
- 1 large egg, whisked
- 1¼ g (½ tsp.) red pepper flakes, crushed
- 125 g (5 C.) fresh baby arugula

Directions:

1. Sizzle oil into a large-sized anti-sticking wok on burner at around medium heat.
2. Cook the kale, shallot, salt and pepper for around 4-5 minutes.
3. Take off from burner and transfer the kale mixture into a large-sized basin.
4. Set aside to cool slightly.
5. With a knife, chop 115 g (4 oz.) of salmon and transfer into the basin of kale mixture.
6. Put the remnant salmon into an electric food processor and process to cut up finely.
7. Transfer the finely cut up salmon into the basin of kale mixture.
8. Put the remnant ingredients and blend to incorporate thoroughly.
9. Make 5 equal-sized patties from the mixture.
10. Lightly spray a large-sized anti-sticking wok with baking spray and sizzle on burner at around medium heat.
11. Cook the patties for around 5 minutes.
12. Carefully flip the patties and cook for around 5 minutes further.
13. Enjoy right away alongside the arugula.

Chicken Kabobs

Servings|6   Time|25 minutes
Nutritional Content (per serving):
Cal| 202   Fat| 9.9g   Protein| 21.7g   Carbs| 6.3g   Fibre| 2.1g

Ingredients:

- ❖ Olive oil baking spray
- ❖ 45 ml (3 tbsp.) olive oil
- ❖ 2 garlic cloves, minced
- ❖ Pinch of sea salt
- ❖ 570 g (1¼ lb.) boneless & skinless chicken breasts, cut into 1-inch cubes
- ❖ Olive oil baking spray
- ❖ 30 g (¼ C.) reduced-fat Parmesan cheese, grated
- ❖ 20 g (1 C.) fresh basil leaves, cut up
- ❖ Powdered black pepper, as desired
- ❖ 2 large capsicums, seeded and cubed
- ❖ 24 cherry tomatoes

Directions:

1. Put the cheese, oil, garlic, basil, salt and pepper into an electric food processor and process to form a smooth mixture.
2. Transfer the basil mixture into a basin.
3. Put the cubed chicken into the basin of basil mixture and toss to incorporate.
4. With a plastic wrap, cover the basin of chicken mixture and put into your fridge to marinate for at least 4-5 hours.
5. For preheating: set your grill to medium-high heat.
6. Generously spray the grill grate with baking spray.
7. Thread the chicken, capsicum and tomatoes onto the pre-soaked wooden skewers.
8. Arrange the skewers onto the grill and cook for around 6-8 minutes, flipping from time to time.
9. Take off the skewers from grill and place onto a platter for around 5 minutes before enjoying.

Stuffed Capsicums

Servings|4   Time|40 minutes
Nutritional Content (per serving):
Cal| 141   Fat| 7.5g   Protein| 2.5g   Carbs| 19.4g   Fibre| 4.5g

Ingredients:

- ❖ Olive oil baking spray
- ❖ 100 g (1 C.) celery
- ❖ 2 garlic cloves, peeled
- ❖ Pinch of sea salt
- ❖ 4 small capsicums, halved and seeded

- ❖ 225 g (8 oz.) fresh mushrooms
- ❖ 60 g (½ C.) onion, roughly cut up
- ❖ 30 ml (2 tbsp.) olive oil
- ❖ Powdered black pepper, as desired

Directions:

1. For preheating: set your oven at 205 °C (400 °F).
2. Spray a baking tray with baking spray.
3. Put the mushrooms, celery, onion, garlic, oil and pepper into an electric food processor and process to cut up finely.
4. Stuff the capsicums with the mushroom mixture into the capsicums.
5. Arrange the capsicums onto the baking tray.
6. Bake for around 20-25 minutes.
7. Enjoy moderately hot.

Egg Drop Soup

Servings|6   Time|30 minutes
Nutritional Content (per serving):
Cal| 80   Fat| 16.1g   Protein| 7.7g   Carbs| 2.6g   Fibre| 0.2g

Ingredients:

- 15 ml (1 tbsp.) olive oil
- 1440 ml (6 C.) salt-free chicken broth, divided
- 90 ml (1/3 C.) fresh lemon juice
- 25 g (¼ C.) green onion (green part), cut up

- 2 garlic cloves, minced
- 2 large eggs
- 10 g (1 tbsp.) arrowroot powder
- Pinch of sea salt
- Ground white pepper, as desired

Directions:

1. Sizzle oil into a large-sized soup pot on burner at around medium heat.
2. Cook the garlic for around 1 minute.
3. Put 1320 ml (5½ C.) of broth and turn the heat at around high.
4. Cook the mixture until boiling.
5. Turn the heat at around medium.
6. Cook for around 5 minutes.
7. In the meantime, put the egg whites, arrowroot powder, lemon juice, white pepper and remnant broth into a basin and whisk to incorporate thoroughly.
8. Slowly Put the egg mixture in the pan, stirring all the time.
9. Simmer for around 5-6 minutes, stirring all the time.
10. Enjoy right away with the garnishing of green onion.

Sweet Potato Soup

Servings|6   Time|1 hour
Nutritional Content (per serving):
Cal| 289   Fat| 16.2g   Protein| 7g   Carbs| 39g   Fibre| 6g

Ingredients:

- 45 ml (3 tbsp.) olive oil
- 130 g (1 C.) raw unsalted cashews
- 10 g (2 tbsp.) fresh ginger root, finely cut up
- 2½ g (1 tsp.) powdered coriander
- 2½ g (1 tsp.) powdered turmeric
- Pinch of sea salt
- 1440 ml (6 C.) salt-free vegetable broth

- 1 large onion, finely cut up
- 1 garlic clove, finely cut up
- 910 g (2 lb.) sweet potatoes, peeled & cut up into ½-inch size
- 2½ g (1 tsp.) powdered cumin
- 2½ g (1 tsp.) cayenne pepper powder
- Powdered black pepper, as desired

Directions:

1. Sizzle oil into a large-sized soup pot on burner at around medium heat.
2. Cook the onion for around 5-6 minutes.
3. Blend in cashews and cook for around 3 minutes.
4. Blend in garlic and ginger and cook for around 1 minute.
5. Blend in remnant ingredients and turn the heat at around high.
6. Cook the mixture until boiling.
7. Turn the heat at around low.
8. Cook with a cover for around 25-30 minutes.
9. Take off the pot of soup from burner and with an immersion blender, puree the soup to incorporate thoroughly.
10. Enjoy right away.

Carrot Soup

Servings|4   Time|50 minutes
Nutritional Content (per serving):
Cal| 121   Fat| 4.4g   Protein| 4.1g   Carbs| 17.2g   Fibre| 3.8g

Ingredients:

- 15 ml (1 tbsp.) olive oil
- 2 garlic cloves, minced
- 5 g (1 tbsp.) fresh ginger root, sliced
- 2 lemongrass stalks
- 480 ml (2 C.) salt-free vegetable broth
- Powdered black pepper, as desired

- 1 medium onion, cut up
- 1 long red chili, cut up
- 520 g (4 C.) carrots, peeled & cut up
- 480 ml (2 C.) filtered water
- Pinch of sea salt
- 2½ g (2 tbsp.) fresh coriander, cut up

Directions:

1. Sizzle oil into a large-sized soup pot on burner at around medium heat.
2. Cook the onion for around 5 minutes.
3. Put in garlic, red chili and ginger and cook for around 5 minutes.
4. Put in carrots, lemongrass stalks, water, broth, salt and pepper and turn the heat at around high.
5. Cook the mixture until boiling.
6. Turn the heat at around low.
7. Cook for around 15-20 minutes.
8. Take off the pot of soup from burner and discard the lemongrass stalks.
9. With a hand blender, blend the soup to form a smooth mixture.
10. Enjoy right away with the garnishing of coriander.

Shrimp in Citrus Sauce

Servings|4   Time|30 minutes
Nutritional Content (per serving):
Cal| 298   Fat| 13.1g   Protein| 29.7g   Carbs| 15.9g   Fibre| 5.7g

Ingredients:

- ❖ 2 large egg whites
- ❖ 35 g (¼ C.) cornstarch
- ❖ Powdered black pepper, as desired
- ❖ 30 ml (2 tbsp.) olive oil
- ❖ 180 ml (¾ C.) fresh orange juice
- ❖ 5 g (1 tsp.) raw honey

- ❖ 30 g (3 tbsp.) sesame seeds
- ❖ Pinch of sea salt
- ❖ 455 g (1 lb.) shrimp, peeled & deveined
- ❖ 60 ml (¼ C.) salt-free chicken broth
- ❖ 30 ml (2 tbsp.) fresh lime juice
- ❖ 1 green onion, thinly sliced

Directions:

1. Put the egg whites, sesame seeds, cornstarch, salt and pepper into a basin and whisk to incorporate thoroughly.
2. Put the in shrimp and toss to incorporate.
3. Sizzle oil into a large-sized wok on burner at around medium heat.
4. Cook the shrimp for around 1-2 minutes per side.
5. Transfer the shrimp onto a large-sized plate.
6. Put the broth and remnant ingredients except for the green onion in the same wok and Cook the mixture until boiling.
7. Cook for around 4-5 minutes, stirring from time to time.
8. Blend in shrimp and cook for around 1-2 minutes.
9. Enjoy right away with the topping of green onion.

Scallops in Yoghurt Sauce

Servings|4   Time|28 minutes
Nutritional Content (per serving):
Cal| 227   Fat| 8.2g   Protein| 26.3g   Carbs| 12.3g   Fibre| 2.7g

Ingredients:

- ❖ 30 ml (2 tbsp.) olive oil
- ❖ 2 tomatoes, finely cut up
- ❖ 2 garlic cloves, minced
- ❖ ¾ g (¼ tsp.) powdered cumin
- ❖ Pinch of sea salt
- ❖ 455 g (1 lb.) sea scallops, side muscles removed
- ❖ 2½ g (2 tbsp.) fresh coriander, cut up

- ❖ 60 g (½ C.) shallot, minced
- ❖ 5 g (1 tbsp.) fresh ginger root, minced
- ❖ ¾ g (¼ tsp.) powdered cinnamon
- ❖ Pinch of cayenne pepper powder
- ❖ Powdered black pepper, as desired
- ❖ 225 g (8 oz.) reduced-fat plain Greek yoghurt, whipped

Directions:

1. Sizzle oil into a large-sized wok on burner at around medium-high heat.
2. Cook the shallots for around 2-3 minutes.
3. Put in tomatoes, spices, salt and pepper and cook for around 3-5 minutes, stirring regularly.
4. Blend in scallops and yoghurt and cook for around 5 minutes.
5. Enjoy right away with the garnishing of coriander.

Dinner Recipes

Turkey & Cabbage Soup

Servings|6   Time|1 hour
Nutritional Content (per serving):
Cal| 210   Fat| 6.7g   Protein| 25.7g   Carbs| 10.8g   Fibre| 3.4g

Ingredients:

- 15 ml (1 tbsp.) olive oil
- 455 g (1 lb.) extra-lean ground turkey
- 5 g (1 tbsp.) fresh ginger root, minced
- Powdered black pepper, as desired
- 600 g (6 C.) cabbage, shredded
- 1 g (½ tsp.) dried thyme
- 1 bay leaf
- 1¼ g (½ tsp.) powdered cumin
- 1440 ml (6 C.) salt-free chicken broth
- 1 large onion, cut up
- 2 garlic cloves, minced
- Pinch of sea salt
- 600 g (6 C.) cabbage, shredded
- 500 g (2½ C.) tomatoes, finely cut up
- 1 g (½ tsp.) dried oregano
- 1¼ g (½ tsp.) paprika
- 1¼ g (½ tsp.) powdered coriander

Directions:

1. Sizzle oil into a large-sized soup pot on burner at around medium-high heat.
2. Cook the onion for around 3-5 minutes.
3. Blend in ground turkey, garlic, ginger, salt and pepper and turn the heat at around medium-high.
4. Cook for around 7-9 minutes.
5. Blend in cabbage, tomatoes, herbs, bay leaf, spices and broth.
6. Cook the mixture until boiling.
7. Turn the heat at around low.
8. Cook for around 25 minutes.
9. Enjoy right away.

Salmon & Quinoa Soup

Servings|8   Time|1½ hours
Nutritional Content (per serving):
Cal| 231   Fat| 7.7g   Protein| 20.5g   Carbs| 15.2g   Fibre| 2.7g

Ingredients:

- 240 g (2 C.) onions, cut up
- 2 garlic cloves, cut up
- 100 g (1 C.) fresh mushrooms, sliced
- 1920-2160 ml (8-9 C.) salt-free chicken broth
- 240 g (8 C.) fresh spinach
- Pinch of sea salt
- 2 green onions, cut up
- 100 g (1 C.) celery, cut up
- 10 g (2 tbsp.) fresh ginger root, finely cut up
- 190 g (1 C.) quinoa, rinsed
- 8 (85-g) (3-oz.) salmon fillets
- 10 g (½ C.) fresh coriander, cut up
- Powdered black pepper, as desired

Directions:

1. Put the onions, celery, garlic, ginger, mushrooms and broth into a large-sized soup pot on burner at around high heat.
2. Cook the mixture until boiling.
3. Put in quinoa and again cook the mixture until boiling.
4. Turn the heat at around low.
5. Cook with the cover for around 45-50 minutes.
6. Arrange the salmon fillets over soup mixture.
7. Cook with the cover for around 10 minutes.
8. Blend in spinach, coriander and salt and cook for around 5 minutes.
9. Enjoy right away with the garnishing of green onions.

Chicken & Spinach Stew

Servings|6   Time|50 minutes
Nutritional Content (per serving):
Cal| 323   Fat| 18.1g   Protein| 27.7g   Carbs| 10.9g   Fibre| 2.9g

Ingredients:

- 30 ml (2 tbsp.) olive oil
- 3 garlic cloves, minced
- 2½ g (1 tsp.) powdered turmeric
- 2½ g (1 tsp.) powdered coriander
- 20 oz. boneless & skinless chicken thighs, cut into 1-inch pieces
- Pinch of sea salt
- 180 g (6 C.) fresh spinach, cut up
- 1 medium onion, cut up
- 5 g (1 tbsp.) fresh ginger root, minced
- 2½ g (1 tsp.) powdered cumin
- 2½ g (1 tsp.) paprika
- 4 large tomatoes, cut up
- 480 ml (2 C.) salt-free chicken broth
- Powdered black pepper, as desired
- 30 ml (2 tbsp.) fresh lemon juice

Directions:

1. Sizzle oil into a large-sized, heavy-bottomed pot on burner at around medium heat.
2. Cook the onion for around 3-4 minutes.
3. Put in ginger, garlic and spices and cook for around 1 minute.
4. Put in chicken and cook for around 4-5 minutes.
5. Put in tomatoes, broth, salt and pepper and turn the heat at around high.
6. Cook the mixture until boiling.
7. Turn the heat at around low.
8. Cook with the cover for around 10-15 minutes.
9. Put the in spinach and cook for around 4-5 minutes.
10. Blend in lemon juice and enjoy right away.

Barley & Lentil Stew

Servings|8   Time|1 hour 10 minutes
Nutritional Content (per serving):
Cal| 264   Fat| 5.8g   Protein| 14.3g   Carbs| 41.2g   Fibre| 14.1g

Ingredients:

- 30 ml (2 tbsp.) olive oil
- 1 large onion, cut up
- 2 garlic cloves, minced
- 2½ g (1 tsp.) powdered cumin
- 220 g (1 C.) barley
- 1000 g (5 C.) tomatoes, finely cut up
- 180 g (6 C.) fresh spinach, torn
- Powdered black pepper, as desired

- 2 carrots, peeled & cut up
- 2 celery stalks, cut up
- 2½ g (1 tsp.) powdered coriander
- 2½ g (1 tsp.) cayenne pepper powder
- 210 g (1 C.) red lentils, rinsed
- 1440 ml (6 C.) salt-free vegetable broth
- Pinch of sea salt

Directions:

1. Sizzle oil into a large-sized pot on burner at around medium heat.
2. Cook the carrots, onion and celery for around 5 minutes.
3. Put the in garlic and spices and cook for around 1 minute.
4. Put in barley, lentils, tomatoes and broth and turn the heat at high.
5. Cook the mixture until boiling.
6. Turn the heat at around low.
7. Cook with the cover for around 40 minutes.
8. Blend in spinach, salt and pepper and cook for around 3-4 minutes.
9. Enjoy right away.

Turkey & Beans Chili

Servings|6   Time|1 hour
Nutritional Content (per serving):
Cal| 301   Fat| 11.1g   Protein| 20.7g   Carbs| 30.2g   Fibre| 7.3g

Ingredients:

- ❖ 30 ml (2 tbsp.) olive oil
- ❖ 1 medium onion, cut up
- ❖ 455 g (1 lb.) extra-lean ground turkey
- ❖ 2½ g (1 tsp.) powdered cumin
- ❖ 480 ml (2 C.) filtered water
- ❖ 5 g (¼ C.) fresh coriander, cut up

- ❖ 1 large capsicum, seeded & cut up
- ❖ 2 garlic cloves, finely cut up
- ❖ 600 g (3 C.) tomatoes, cut up
- ❖ 1¼ g (½ tsp.) powdered turmeric
- ❖ 1 (510-g) (18-oz.) can no-salt-added black beans, rinsed & drained

Directions:

1. Sizzle oil into a large-sized pot on burner at around medium heat.
2. Cook the capsicum, onion and garlic for around 5 minutes.
3. Blend in turkey and cook for around 5 minutes.
4. Blend in tomatoes, beans, spices and water and turn the heat at around high.
5. Cook the mixture until boiling.
6. Turn the heat at around medium-low heat and blend in beans.
7. Cook with cover for around 30 minutes, stirring from time to time.
8. Enjoy right away with the garnishing of coriander.

Chickpeas & Courgette Curry

Servings|6   Time|50 minutes
Nutritional Content (per serving):
Cal| 213   Fat| 10.1g   Protein| 12.7g   Carbs| 24.2g   Fibre| 7g

Ingredients:

- 30 ml (2 tbsp.) olive oil
- 2 garlic cloves, minced
- 2½ g (1 tsp.) powdered coriander
- 1¼ g (½ tsp.) powdered turmeric
- Pinch of sea salt
- 2 large courgettes, sliced
- 2 (15-oz.) (425-g) cans no-salt-added chickpeas, rinsed & drained

- 1 medium onion, finely cut up
- 10 g (2 tbsp.) fresh ginger root, minced
- 2½ g (1 tsp.) powdered cumin
- 1¼ g (½ tsp.) cayenne pepper powder
- Powdered black pepper, as desired
- 2 large tomatoes, finely cut up
- 480 ml (2 C.) filtered water
- 5 g (¼ C.) fresh parsley, cut up

Directions:

1. Sizzle oil into a large-sized pot on burner at around medium heat.
2. Cook the onion, garlic and ginger for 6-8 minutes.
3. Blend in spices cook for around 1-2 minutes.
4. Blend in courgette and tomatoes and cook for around 3-5 minutes.
5. Blend in chickpeas and water and turn the heat at around high.
6. Cook the mixture until boiling.
7. Turn the heat at around medium and cook for around 10-15 minutes.
8. Enjoy right away with a garnish of parsley.

Chicken & Cauliflower Curry

Servings|6   Time|35 minutes
Nutritional Content (per serving):
Cal| 243   Fat| 21.1g   Protein| 28.7g   Carbs| 8.2g   Fibre| 3.7g

Ingredients:

- 30 ml (2 tbsp.) olive oil
- 15 g (2 tbsp.) curry powder
- Pinch of sea salt
- Powdered black pepper, as desired
- 1 capsicum, seeded & cut up
- 480 ml (2 C.) salt-free chicken broth
- 3 garlic cloves, finely cut up
- 680 g (1½ lb.) boneless chicken thighs, cut into bite-sized pieces
- 455 g (1 lb.) cauliflower, cut into small florets
- 5 g (¼ C.) fresh parsley, cut up

Directions:

1. Sizzle oil into a large-sized wok on burner at around medium heat.
2. Cook the garlic and curry powder for around 1 minute.
3. Put in chicken, salt and pepper and cook for around 5-6 minutes, stirring frequently.
4. With a slotted spoon, transfer the chicken onto a plate.
5. Put the cauliflower and capsicum into the wok and cook for around 2-3 minutes.
6. Put in broth and cook for around 5-7 minutes.
7. Blend in cooked chicken, salt and pepper and cook for around 2-3 minutes.
8. Enjoy right away with the garnishing of parsley.

Chicken in Dill Sauce

Servings|6   Time|1¼ hours
Nutritional Content (per serving):
Cal| 279   Fat| 21.1g   Protein| 36.7g   Carbs| 4.5g   Fibre| 0.7g

Ingredients:

- 30 ml (2 tbsp.) olive oil
- 1 small onion, sliced
- 8 fresh dill sprigs
- 1¼ g (½ tsp.) powdered turmeric
- Powdered black pepper, as desired
- 15 g (2 tbsp.) cornstarch
- 2½ g (2 tbsp.) fresh dill, cut up

- 6 skinless & bone-in chicken thighs
- 960 ml (4 C.) salt-free chicken broth
- 1¼ g (½ tsp.) cayenne pepper powder
- Pinch of sea salt
- 30 ml (2 tbsp.) fresh lemon juice
- 15 ml (1 tbsp.) cold water

Directions:

1. Sizzle oil into a large-sized Dutch oven on burner at around high heat.
2. Put the chicken thighs into the pot and cook for around 4 minutes.
3. Transfer the chicken thighs onto a plate.
4. Put the onion in the same pot on burner at around medium heat.
5. Cook for around 5-7 minutes.
6. Put the chicken thighs and sprinkle with cayenne pepper powder and turmeric.
7. Pour the broth and dill sprigs on top and turn the heat at around medium-high.
8. Cook the mixture until boiling.
9. Turn the heat at around medium-low.
10. Cook with the cover for around 40-45 minutes, coating the thighs with cooking liquid from time to time.
11. Discard the thyme sprigs and transfer the thighs into a basin.
12. Put the lemon juice, salt and pepper and blend to incorporate.
13. In a small-sized basin, dissolve the cornstarch into water.
14. Slowly put the cornstarch mixture into the pan, stirring all the time.
15. Cook for around 3-4 minutes, stirring frequently.
16. Pour sauce over thighs and enjoy right away with a sprinkling of cut up dill.

Turkey & Mushroom Bake

Servings|8   Time|3¼ hours
Nutritional Content (per serving):
Cal| 189   Fat| 3.4g   Protein| 26.7g   Carbs| 13.2g   Fibre| 3.1g

Ingredients:

- 240 ml (1 C.) filtered water
- 680 g (1½ lb.) boneless turkey meat, cubed
- 600 g (3 C.) tomatoes, cut up
- 2 medium onions, cut up
- 1¼ g (1 tbsp.) fresh thyme, cut up
- 480 ml (2 C.) salt-free chicken broth
- Powdered black pepper, as desired
- 10 g (3 tbsp.) arrowroot starch
- 455 g (1 lb.) fresh mushrooms, sliced
- 4 medium carrots, peeled & cut up
- 2 celery stalks, cut up
- 2 garlic cloves, finely cut up
- Pinch of sea salt

Directions:

1. For preheating: set your oven at 165 °C (325 °F).
2. Put the water and arrowroot starch into a small-sized basin and blend to incorporate thoroughly.
3. Put the turkey cubes and remnant ingredients into a large-sized ovenproof pot and blend to incorporate.
4. Put the arrowroot starch mixture and blend to incorporate.
5. Cover the pot and bake for around 3 hours, stirring after every 30 minutes.
6. Enjoy right away.

Ground Turkey with Lentils

Servings|4   Time|1¼ hours
Nutritional Content (per serving):
Cal| 378   Fat| 11.1g   Protein| 35.7g   Carbs| 32.2g   Fibre| 14.7g

Ingredients:

- 15 ml (1 tbsp.) olive oil
- 455 g (1 lb.) extra-lean ground turkey
- 2 garlic cloves, minced
- 1 jalapeño pepper, seeded & cut up
- 210 g (1 C.) red lentils, rinsed
- 5 g (2 tsp.) paprika
- Pinch of sea salt
- 1200 ml (5 C.) salt-free chicken broth

- 1 small onion, cut up
- 1 carrot, peeled & cut up
- 5 g (1 tbsp.) fresh ginger root, minced
- 400 g (2 C.) tomatoes, cut up
- 2 g (1 tsp.) dried oregano
- 5 g (2 tsp.) powdered cumin
- Powdered black pepper, as desired

Directions:

1. Sizzle oil into a large-sized Dutch oven on burner at around medium heat.
2. Cook the onion for around 3-4 minutes.
3. Put in ground turkey and cook for around 4-5 minutes.
4. Put in carrot, garlic, ginger and jalapeño pepper and cook for around 1 minutes, stirring from time to time.
5. Blend in remnant ingredients and tur the heat at around high.
6. Cook the mixture until boiling.
7. Turn the heat at around low.
8. Cook with the cover for around 40-50 minutes, stirring from time to time.
9. Enjoy right away.

Orange Poached Salmon

Servings|3   Time|30 minutes
Nutritional Content (per serving):
Cal| 260   Fat| 10.1g   Protein| 33.7g   Carbs| 7.5g   Fibre| 0.2g

Ingredients:

- 3 garlic cloves
- 90 ml (1/3 C.) fresh orange juice
- 20 g (1 tbsp.) raw honey
- Powdered black pepper, as desired
- 2½ g (½ tbsp.) fresh ginger root, grated finely
- Pinch of sea salt
- 3 (170-g) (6-oz.) salmon fillets

Directions:

1. Put the garlic, ginger, orange juice, honey, salt and pepper into a medium-sized basin and blend to incorporate.
2. Put the salmon fillets in the bottom of a large-sized pot and top with ginger mixture.
3. Set aside for around 15 minutes.
4. Put the pot on burner at around high heat.
5. Cook the mixture until boiling.
6. Turn the heat at around low.
7. Cook with the cover for around 10-12 minutes.
8. Enjoy right away.

Salmon with Yoghurt Sauce

Servings|4   Time|25 minutes
Nutritional Content (per serving):
Cal| 312   Fat| 17.1g   Protein| 33.7g   Carbs| 1.4g   Fibre| 0.1g

Ingredients:

- ❖ Olive oil baking spray
- ❖ 1¼ g (½ tsp.) powdered coriander
- ❖ 1¼ g (½ tsp.) powdered turmeric
- ❖ 1¼ g (½ tsp.) cayenne pepper powder
- ❖ Powdered black pepper, as desired

- ❖ 65 g (¼ C.) reduced-fat plain Greek yoghurt
- ❖ 1¼ g (½ tsp.) powdered ginger
- ❖ Pinch of sea salt
- ❖ 4 (170-g) (6-oz.) skinless salmon fillets

Directions:

1. For preheating: set your oven to broiler. Spray a broiler pan with baking spray.
2. Put the yoghurt, spices, salt and pepper into a basin and blend to incorporate.
3. Arrange salmon fillets onto the broiler pan into a single layer.
4. Put the yoghurt mixture over each fillet.
5. Broil for around 12-14 minutes.

Cod & Mushroom Casserole

Servings|4   Time|35 minutes
Nutritional Content (per serving):
Cal| 182   Fat| 7.1g   Protein| 21.7g   Carbs| 1.6g   Fibre| 0.5g

Ingredients:

- ❖ 30 ml (2 tbsp.) olive oil
- ❖ 150 g (1½ C.) fresh mushrooms, sliced
- ❖ Pinch of sea salt
- ❖ 2 g (1 tsp.) dried thyme, crushed

- ❖ 30 g (¼ C.) onion, cut up
- ❖ 455 g (1 lb.) cod fillets
- ❖ Powdered black pepper, as desired

Directions:

1. For preheating: set your oven at 230 ºC (450 ºF).
2. Into a wok, melt margarine on burner at around medium heat.
3. Cook the onion and mushrooms for around 5-6 minutes.
4. Arrange the cod fillets into a large-sized baking pan and top with the mushroom mixture.
5. Sprinkle with black pepper and thyme
6. Bake for around 12-15 minutes.

Shrimp Casserole

Servings|6   Time|50 minutes
Nutritional Content (per serving):
Cal| 272   Fat| 13.2g   Protein| 29.7g   Carbs| 6g   Fibre| 1g

Ingredients:

- 60 ml (¼ C.) olive oil
- 680 g (1½ lb.) shrimp, peeled & deveined
- 1 g (½ tsp.) dried thyme, crushed
- 1¼ g (½ tsp.) red pepper flakes, crushed
- 120 ml (½ C.) salt-free chicken broth
- 500 g (2½ C.) tomatoes, cut up
- 3 garlic cloves, minced
- 1 g (½ tsp.) dried oregano, crushed
- 5 g (¼ C.) fresh parsley, cut up
- 15 ml (1 tbsp.) fresh lemon juice
- 115 g (4 oz.) reduced-fat feta cheese, crumbled

Directions:

1. For preheating: set your oven at 175 °C (350 °F).
2. Sizzle oil into a large-sized wok on burner at around medium-high heat.
3. Cook the garlic for around 1 minute.
4. Put in shrimp, oregano, thyme and red pepper flakes and cook for around 4-5 minutes.
5. Blend in parsley and salt and immediately transfer into a casserole dish.
6. Put the broth and lemon juice in the same wok on burner at around medium heat.
7. Cook for around 2-3 minutes.
8. Blend in tomatoes and cook for around 2-3 minutes.
9. Pour the tomato mixture over shrimp mixture and sprinkle with cheese.
10. Bake for around 15-20 minutes.
11. Take off from the oven and enjoy right away.

Lentil & Rice Bake

Servings|6   Time|1¼ hours
Nutritional Content (per serving):
Cal| 192   Fat| 1.5g   Protein| 11.4g   Carbs| 34.5g   Fibre| 12.1g

Ingredients:

- 600 ml (2½ C.) filtered water, divided
- 80 g (½ C.) wild rice, rinsed
- 1 small onion, cut up
- 40 g (1/3 C.) courgette, cut up
- 40 g (1/3 C.) celery, cut up
- 225 g (8 oz.) salt-free tomato puree
- 1¼ g (½ tsp.) powdered turmeric
- 2 g (1 tsp.) dried basil
- Powdered black pepper, as desired

- 210 g (1 C.) red lentils, rinsed
- 5 ml (1 tsp.) olive oil
- 3 garlic cloves, finely cut up
- 50 g (1/3 C.) carrot, peeled & cut up
- 1 medium tomato, cut up
- 2½ g (1 tsp.) powdered cumin
- 2 g (1 tsp.) dried oregano
- Pinch of sea salt

Directions:

1. Put 240 ml (1 C.) of water and rice into a pot on burner at around medium-high heat.
2. Cook the mixture until boiling.
3. Turn the heat at around low.
4. Cook with a cover for around 20 minutes.
5. In the meantime, put the remnant water and lentils into another pot on burner at around medium-high heat.
6. Cook the mixture until boiling.
7. Turn the heat at around low.
8. Cook with a cover for around 15 minutes.
9. Shift the cooked rice and lentils into a casserole dish and set aside.
10. For preheating: set your oven at 175 °C (350 °F).
11. Sizzle oil into a large-sized wok on burner at around medium heat.
12. Cook the onion and garlic for around 4-5 minutes.
13. Blend in courgette, carrot, celery, tomato and tomato puree and cook for around 4-5 minutes.
14. Blend in cumin, herbs, salt and pepper and take off from burner.
15. Shift the vegetable mixture into the casserole dish with rice and lentils and blend to incorporate.
16. Bake for around 30 minutes.
17. Take off the casserole dish from your oven and set aside for around 5 minutes before enjoying.

Drinks & Teas Recipes

Citrus Detox Water

Servings|3   Time|10 minutes
Nutritional Content (per serving):
Cal| 41   Fat| 0.2g   Protein| 1.1g   Carbs| 10.4g   Fibre| 2.5g

Ingredients:

- 1 orange, sliced
- 1 lemon, sliced
- 2½ g (2 tbsp.) fresh mint leaves
- 1 lime, sliced
- ½ of cucumber, sliced
- 1440 ml (6 C.) filtered water

Directions:

1. Put the orange, lime, lemon, cucumber and mint leaves into a large-sized glass jar and pour water on top.
2. Cover the jar with a lid and put into your fridge for around 2-4 hours before enjoying.

Strawberry Detox Water

Servings|3   Time|10 minutes
Nutritional Content (per serving):
Cal| 18   Fat| 0.2g   Protein| 0.4g   Carbs| 4.5g   Fibre| 1.4g

Ingredients:

- 125 g (1 C.) fresh strawberries, sliced
- 1¼ g (1 tbsp.) fresh mint leaves
- 1 lemon, sliced
- 1440 ml (6 C.) filtered water

Directions:

1. Put the strawberry, lemon and mint leaves into a large-sized glass jar and pour water on top.
2. Cover the jar with a lid and put into your fridge for around 2-4 hours before enjoying.

Lemonade

Servings|5 Time|10 minutes
Nutritional Content (per serving):
Cal| 131   Fat| 0g   Protein| 0.1g   Carbs| 35.2g   Fibre| 0.7g

Ingredients:

- ❖ 840 ml (3½ C.) filtered water
- ❖ 240 ml (1 C.) fresh lemon juice
- ❖ 150 g (½ C.) raw honey
- ❖ 8-10 Ice cubes

Directions:

1. Put the water and honey into a large-sized pitcher and blend to dissolve.
2. Blend in lemon juice and fill the pitcher with ice.
3. Enjoy chilled.

Orange Juice

Servings|2 Time|10 minutes
Nutritional Content (per serving):
Cal| 250   Fat| 0.9g   Protein| 1.7g   Carbs| 64.2g   Fibre| 13.3g

Ingredients:

- ❖ 6 large oranges, peeled & sectioned
- ❖ Ice cubes, as desired

Directions:

1. Put the orange pieces into a juicer and extract the juice according to manufacturer's directions.
2. Transfer the juice into ice filled glasses and enjoy right away.

Strawberry Juice

Servings|2   Time|10 minutes
Nutritional Content (per serving):
Cal| 46   Fat| 0.4g   Protein| 1g   Carbs| 11.2g   Fibre| 3g

Ingredients:

- ❖ 250 g (2 C.) fresh strawberries, hulled
- ❖ 480 ml (2 C.) chilled water
- ❖ 5 ml (1 tsp.) fresh lime juice

Directions:

1. Put the strawberries, lime juice and water into an electric blender and process until perfectly smooth.
2. Divide the ice cubes into your glasses.
3. Through a fine mesh strainer, strain the juice into glasses and enjoy right away.

Apple & Spinach Juice

Servings|2   Time|10 minutes
Nutritional Content (per serving):
Cal| 196   Fat| 0.6g   Protein| 5.2g   Carbs| 45.9g   Fibre| 8.2g

Ingredients:

- ❖ 2 large green apples, cored & sliced
- ❖ 5 g (¼ C.) fresh parsley leaves
- ❖ 1 lime, peeled & seeded
- ❖ 220 g (4 C.) fresh kale leaves
- ❖ 5 g (1 tbsp.) fresh ginger root, peeled
- ❖ 240 ml (1 C.) chilled water

Directions:

1. Put the apples and remnant ingredients into an electric blender and process until perfectly smooth.
2. Divide the ice cubes into your glasses.
3. Through a fine mesh strainer, strain the juice into glasses and enjoy right away.

Strawberry & Orange Smoothie

Servings|2   Time|10 minutes
Nutritional Content (per serving):
Cal| 95   Fat| 0.7g   Protein| 1.7g   Carbs| 22.7g   Fibre| 3.7g

Ingredients:

- ❖ 190 g (1½ C.) fresh strawberries, hulled
- ❖ 240 ml (1 C.) fresh orange juice
- ❖ 10 g (2 tsp.) raw honey
- ❖ 4-5 ice cubes

Directions:

1. Put the strawberries and remnant ingredients into an electric blender and process to form a smooth and creamy smoothie.
2. Enjoy right away.

Blueberry & Cucumber Smoothie

Servings|2   Time|10 minutes
Nutritional Content (per serving):
Cal| 137   Fat| 1.9g   Protein| 2.7g   Carbs| 20.9g   Fibre| 5.7g

Ingredients:

- ❖ 225 g (1½ C.) frozen blueberries
- ❖ 120 g (1 C.) cucumber, peeled & cut up
- ❖ 360 ml (1½ C.) filtered water
- ❖ 1 small banana, peeled & sliced
- ❖ 10 g (1 tbsp.) chia seeds
- ❖ 4-5 ice cubes

Directions:

1. Put the blueberries and remnant ingredients into an electric blender and process to form a smooth and creamy smoothie.
2. Enjoy right away.

Kale & Avocado Smoothie

Servings|2   Time|10 minutes
Nutritional Content (per serving):
Cal| 239   Fat| 13.1g   Protein| 5.5g   Carbs| 27.8g   Fibre| 6.5g

Ingredients:

- ❖ 110 g (2 C.) fresh kale
- ❖ 40 g (2 tbsp.) raw honey
- ❖ 10 g (1 tbsp.) hemp seeds, shelled
- ❖ ½ avocado, peeled, pitted & cut up
- ❖ 1¼ g (½ tsp.) powdered cinnamon
- ❖ 480 ml (2 C.) chilled water

Directions:

1. Put the kale and remnant ingredients into an electric blender and process to form a smooth and creamy smoothie.
2. Enjoy right away.

Spinach & Lettuce Smoothie

Servings|2   Time|10 minutes
Nutritional Content (per serving):
Cal| 81   Fat| 0.6g   Protein| 1.6g   Carbs| 19.6g   Fibre| 4.7g

Ingredients:

- ❖ 60 g (2 C.) fresh spinach
- ❖ 5 g (¼ C.) fresh mint leaves
- ❖ 25 g (1½ tbsp.) raw honey
- ❖ 4-5 ice cubes
- ❖ 100 g (2 C.) romaine lettuce, cut up
- ❖ 15 ml (1 tbsp.) fresh lemon juice
- ❖ 360 ml (1½ C.) filtered water

Directions:

1. Put the spinach and remnant ingredients into an electric blender and process to form a smooth and creamy smoothie.
2. Enjoy right away.

Chamomile Herbal Tea

Servings|2   Time|10 minutes
Nutritional Content (per serving):
Cal| 68   Fat| 0.2g   Protein| 0.4g   Carbs| 18.2g   Fibre| 3g

Ingredients:

- ❖ 2 thin apple slices
- ❖ 10 g (2 tbsp.) chamomile flowers
- ❖ 480 ml (2 C.) boiling water
- ❖ 10 g (2 tsp.) raw honey

Directions:

1. Rinse the teapot with boiling water.
2. Put the apple slices in the warm pot and with a wooden spoon, mash them.
3. Put the chamomile flowers and top with the boiling water.
4. Cover the pot and steep for 3-5 minutes.
5. Strain the tea into two serving mugs and blend in honey.
6. Enjoy right away.

Ginger & Lime Herbal Tea

Servings|2   Time|25 minutes
Nutritional Content (per serving):
Cal| 34   Fat| 0.1g   Protein| 0.1g   Carbs| 8.6g   Fibre| 0.2g

Ingredients:

- ❖ 560 ml (2¼ C.) filtered water
- ❖ 15 ml (1 tbsp.) fresh lime juice
- ❖ 20 g (1 tbsp.) raw honey
- ❖ 10 g 10 g (2 tbsp.) fresh ginger root, cut into slices

Directions:

1. Put the water, ginger and cinnamon into a pot on burner at around high heat.
2. Cook the mixture until boiling.
3. Turn the heat at around low.
4. Cook for around 10 minutes.
5. Take off from burner and strain the tea into serving mugs.
6. Blend in lime juice and honey and enjoy right away.

Elderberry Herbal Tea

Servings|2   Time|25 minutes
Nutritional Content (per serving):
Cal| 19   Fat| 0.1g   Protein| 0.1g   Carbs| .9g   Fibre| 1.2g

Ingredients:

- 560 ml (2¼ C.) filtered water
- 1¼ g (½ tsp.) powdered turmeric
- 10 g (2 tsp.) pure maple syrup
- 100 g (2 tbsp.) dried elderberries
- ¾ g (¼ tsp.) powdered cinnamon

Directions:

1. Put the water, elderberries, turmeric and cinnamon into a small-sized pot on burner at around medium-high heat.
2. Cook the mixture until boiling.
3. Turn the heat at around low.
4. Cook for around 15 minutes.
5. Take off the pot of tea from burner and set aside to cool for around 5 minutes.
6. Through a fine mesh strainer, strain the tea into serving mugs and blend in maple syrup.

Chilled Green Tea

Servings|2   Time|10 minutes
Nutritional Content (per serving):
Cal| 1   Fat| 0.3g   Protein| 1.7g   Carbs| 9.5g   Fibre| 3.2g

Ingredients:

- 600 ml (2½ C.) boiling water
- 4 green tea bags
- 20 g (1 C.) fresh mint leaves
- 10 g (2 tsp.) raw honey

Directions:

1. Put the water, mint and tea bags into a pitcher and blend to incorporate.
2. Cover and steep for around 5 minutes.
3. Put into your fridge for at least 3 hours.
4. Discard the tea bags and divide the tea into serving glasses.
5. Blend in honey and enjoy.

Lemon Iced Tea

Servings|6   Time|15 minutes
Nutritional Content (per serving):
Cal| 16   Fat| 0.1g   Protein| 0.2g   Carbs| 4.2g   Fibre| 1g

Ingredients:

- ❖ 1440 ml (6 C.) filtered water
- ❖ 5 fresh thyme sprigs
- ❖ 3 black tea bags

- ❖ 60 ml (¼ C.) fresh lemon juice
- ❖ 1 cinnamon stick
- ❖ 15 g (3 tsp.) raw honey

Directions:

1. Put the water, lemon juice, thyme, lemon zest and cinnamon into a large-sized pot on burner at around medium-high heat.
2. Cook the mixture until boiling.
3. Immediately take off the pot from burner and put in tea bags and honey.
4. Cover the pot and set aside for 15 minutes to steep.
5. Take off the tea bags and thyme sprigs and let the tea cool for around an hour.
6. Through a fine mesh strainer, strain the tea mixture into a pitcher.
7. Put into your fridge to chill before enjoying.

Snacks & Appetizer Recipes

Cinnamon Almonds

Servings|8   Time|20 minutes
Nutritional Content (per serving):
Cal| 156   Fat| 13.1g   Protein| 4.7g   Carbs| 5.8g   Fibre| 4.5g

Ingredients:

- ❖ 280 g (2 C.) unsalted whole almonds
- ❖ Pinch of sea salt
- ❖ 2½ g (1 tsp.) powdered cinnamon
- ❖ 15 ml (1 tbsp.) olive oil

Directions:

1. For preheating: set your oven at 175 °C (350 °F).
2. Lay out bakery paper into a baking pan.
3. Put the almonds and remnant ingredients into a medium-sized basin and toss to incorporate thoroughly.
4. Arrange the almonds into the baking pan.
5. Roast for around 10 minutes, flipping once after 5 minutes.
6. Take off the baking pan of almonds from oven and set aside to cool thoroughly before enjoying.

Spiced Chickpeas

Servings|6   Time|35 minutes
Nutritional Content (per serving):
Cal| 248   Fat| 11.1g   Protein| 10.5g   Carbs| 23.6g   Fibre| 6.2g

Ingredients:

- ❖ 2 (15-oz.) (425-g) cans no-salt-added chickpeas, rinsed & drained
- ❖ 1¼ g (½ tsp.) cayenne pepper powder
- ❖ 1¼ g (½ tsp.) powdered turmeric
- ❖ Powdered black pepper, as desired
- ❖ 60 ml (¼ C.) olive oil
- ❖ 1¼ g (½ tsp.) red chili powder
- ❖ 1¼ g (½ tsp.) powdered cumin
- ❖ Pinch of sea salt

Directions:

1. For preheating: set your oven at 220 °C (425 °F).
2. Lay out bakery paper into a large-sized baking pan.
3. Put the chickpeas, oil, spices, salt and pepper into a basin and toss to incorporate thoroughly.
4. Place the chickpeas onto the baking pan and spread in an even layer.
5. Roast for around 20-25 minutes, flipping after every 5 minutes.
6. Enjoy right away.

Apple Chips

Servings|6   Time|2¼ hours
Nutritional Content (per serving):
Cal| 71   Fat| 0.6g   Protein| 0.7g   Carbs| 18.5g   Fibre| 4.5g

Ingredients:
- 5 g (2 tsp.) powdered cinnamon
- 1¼ g (½ tsp.) powdered nutmeg
- 2½ g (1 tsp.) powdered ginger
- 3 Fuji apples, sliced thinly in rounds

Directions:
1. For preheating: set your oven at 95 °C (200 °F).
2. Lay out bakery paper onto a baking tray.
3. Put the spices into a basin and blend to incorporate.
4. Arrange the apple slices onto baking tray and sprinkle with spice mixture generously.
5. Bake for around 1 hour. Flip the side and again sprinkle with spice mixture.
6. Bake for around 1 hour. Take off the baking tray from oven and set aside to cool thoroughly before enjoying.

Spinach Chips

Servings|4   Time|18 minutes
Nutritional Content (per serving):
Cal| 38   Fat| 2.9g   Protein| 1.7g   Carbs| 2.3g   Fibre| 1.4g

Ingredients:
- 120 g (4 C.) fresh spinach leaves
- Pinch of sea salt
- 2½ g (½ tsp.) Italian seasoning
- 10 ml (2 tsp.) olive oil
- 1¼ g (½ tsp.) powdered turmeric

Directions:
1. For preheating: set your oven at 165 °C (325 °F). Lay out bakery paper onto a large-sized baking tray.
2. Put the spinach leaves into a large-sized basin and drizzle with oil.
3. With your hands, rub the spinach leaves until all the leaves are coated with oil.
4. Shift the leaves onto the baking tray and spread in an even layer.
5. Sprinkle the spinach leaves with salt, turmeric and Italian seasoning. Bake for around 8 minutes.
6. Take off the baking tray of chips from oven and set aside for around 5 minutes before enjoying.

Sweet Potato Fries

Servings|2 Time|35 minutes
Nutritional Content (per serving):
Cal| 199   Fat| 12.1g   Protein| 1.7g   Carbs| 18.2g   Fibre| 3.7g

Ingredients:

- 1 large sweet potato, peeled & cut into wedges
- 1¼ g (½ tsp.) powdered turmeric
- Pinch of sea salt
- 30 ml (2 tbsp.) olive oil
- 1¼ g (½ tsp.) paprika
- 1¼ g (½ tsp.) powdered cumin
- Powdered black pepper, as desired

Directions:

1. For preheating: set your oven at 220 °C (425 °F).
2. Lay out a piece of heavy-duty foil onto a large-sized baking tray.
3. Put the sweet potato wedges and remnant ingredients into a large-sized basin and toss to incorporate thoroughly.
4. Transfer the sweet potato wedges onto the baking tray and then spread in an even layer.
5. Bake for around 25 minutes, flipping once after 15 minutes.
6. Take off from the oven and enjoy right away.

Stuffed Cherry Tomatoes

Servings|6 Time|15 minutes
Nutritional Content (per serving):
Cal| 75   Fat| 5.2g   Protein| 1.7g   Carbs| 8.7g   Fibre| 4.4g

Ingredients:

- 340 g (2¼ C.) cherry tomatoes
- 15 g (2 tbsp.) unsalted cashews, cut up
- 1 jalapeño pepper, seeded & cut up
- 15 ml (1 tbsp.) fresh lemon juice
- 1 small avocado, peeled, pitted & cut up
- 2 garlic cloves, cut up
- 2½ g (2 tbsp.) fresh basil leaves

Directions:

1. In
2. With a small-sized knife, cut the top of each tomato.
3. With a little scooper, take off the seeds from tomatoes, to create a cup.
4. Lay out the tomatoes onto large plate, cut side up.
5. Put the avocado and remnant ingredients into an electric food processor and process to incorporate thoroughly.
6. Carefully fill each tomato cup with avocado mixture.

Deviled Eggs

Servings|6   Time|20 minutes
Nutritional Content (per serving):
Cal| 82   Fat| 5.2g   Protein| 7g   Carbs| 1.3g   Fibre| 0.7g

Ingredients:

- ❖ 6 large eggs
- ❖ 2½ g (2 tbsp.) fresh chives, finely cut up
- ❖ 20 g (1 tbsp.) Dijon mustard
- ❖ 65 g (¼ C.) reduced-fat plain Greek yoghurt
- ❖ Pinch of cayenne pepper powder

Directions:

1. Put the eggs into a pot of water on burner at around high heat.
2. Cook the water until boiling. Cover the pot of eggs and immediately take off from burner.
3. Set the pot of eggs aside with the cover for at least 10-15 minutes.
4. Drain the eggs and let them cool thoroughly.
5. Peel the eggs and, with a sharp knife, slice them in half vertically
6. Take off the yolks from egg halves. Carefully scoop out the yolks from each egg half.
7. Into a clean processor Put the egg yolks and yoghurt and process until perfectly smooth. Put the yoghurt mixture into a basin.
8. Put the in the green onion greens, chives and mustard and blend to incorporate.
9. Spoon the yoghurt mixture in each egg half. Enjoy with a sprinkling of cayenne pepper powder.

Avocado Guacamole

Servings|4   Time|10 minutes
Nutritional Content (per serving):
Cal| 217   Fat| 18.1g   Protein| 2.4g   Carbs| 11.3g   Fibre| 7.4g

Ingredients:

- ❖ 2 medium avocados, peeled, pitted, & cut up
- ❖ 1 Serrano pepper, seeded & cut up
- ❖ 2½ g (2 tbsp.) fresh coriander, cut up
- ❖ Pinch of sea salt
- ❖ 1 small red onion, cut up
- ❖ 1 garlic clove, minced
- ❖ 1 tomato, seeded & cut up
- ❖ 15 ml (1 tbsp.) fresh lime juice

Directions:

1. Put the avocado into a large-sized basin and with a fork, mash it thoroughly.
2. Put in remnant ingredients and gently blend to incorporate.
3. Enjoy right away.

Strawberry Salsa

Servings|4   Time|15 minutes
Nutritional Content (per serving):
Cal| 44   Fat| 0.3g   Protein| 0.9g   Carbs| 11.2g   Fibre| 2.7g

Ingredients:

- 250 g (2 C.) fresh strawberries, hulled & sliced
- 5 g (1 tsp.) raw honey
- ½ small red onion, cut up
- Pinch of sea salt
- 30 ml (2 tbsp.) fresh lime juice
- 1 jalapeño pepper, seeded & cut up
- 10 g (½ C.) fresh coriander, cut up
- Powdered black pepper, as desired

Directions:

1. Put the strawberries and remnant ingredients into a large-sized serving dish and gently blend to incorporate.
2. Enjoy right away.

Berries Gazpacho

Servings|6   Time|15 minutes
Nutritional Content (per serving):
Cal| 177   Fat| 0.7g   Protein| 4.7g   Carbs| 37.2g   Fibre| 5.6g

Ingredients:

- 500 g (2 C.) reduced-fat plain Greek yoghurt
- 75 g (¼ C.) raw honey
- 120 ml (½ C.) fresh orange juice
- 910 g (2 lb.) fresh mixed berries
- 5 ml (1 tsp.) organic vanilla extract

Directions:

1. Put the yoghurt and remnant ingredients into an electric blender and process to form a smooth mixture.
2. Transfer the mixture into a large-sized serving dish.
3. Cover the dish and put into your fridge to chill for at least 2-3 hours before enjoying.

Dessert Recipes

Strawberry Ice Cream

Servings|6   Time|10 minutes
Nutritional Content (per serving):
Cal| 143   Fat| 4.1g   Protein| 1.7g   Carbs| 28.5g   Fibre| 4.4g

Ingredients:

- ❖ 4 medium frozen bananas, peeled
- ❖ ½ of avocado, peeled, pitted & cut up
- ❖ 20 g (1 tbsp.) raw honey
- ❖ 125 g (1 C.) frozen strawberries
- ❖ 60 ml (¼ C.) unsweetened almond milk

Directions:

1. Put the bananas and remnant ingredients into an electric blender and process to form a smooth mixture.
2. Transfer the mixture into an airtight container and put into your fridge for around 4-6 hours before enjoying.

Spinach Sorbet

Servings|4   Time|15 minutes
Nutritional Content (per serving):
Cal| 166   Fat| 15.1g   Protein| 2.4g   Carbs| 5.8g   Fibre| 3.3g

Ingredients:

- ❖ 90 g (3 C.) fresh spinach, torn
- ❖ ½ of avocado, peeled, pitted & cut up
- ❖ 40 g (2 tbsp.) raw honey
- ❖ 5 ml (1 tsp.) organic vanilla extract
- ❖ 8-10 ice cubes
- ❖ 1¼ g (1 tbsp.) fresh basil leaves
- ❖ 180 ml (¾ C.) unsweetened almond milk
- ❖ 5 g (1 tsp.) unsalted almonds, cut up very finely

Directions:

1. Put the spinach and remnant ingredients into an electric blender and process until creamy and smooth.
2. Transfer into an ice cream maker and process according to manufacturer's directions.
3. Transfer into an airtight container and freeze for at least 4-5 hours before enjoying.

Mixed Berries Granita

Servings|4   Time|15 minutes
Nutritional Content (per serving):
Cal| 46   Fat| 0.3g   Protein| 0.7g   Carbs| 11.2g   Fibre| 2.9g

Ingredients:

- ❖ 280 g (2 C.) fresh mixed berries
- ❖ 15 ml (1 tbsp.) fresh lemon juice
- ❖ 20 g (1 tbsp.) pure maple syrup
- ❖ 8-10 ice cubes

Directions:

1. Put the berries, maple syrup, lemon juice and ice cubes into an electric blender and process to form a smooth mixture.
2. Transfer the berry mixture into an 8x8-inch baking pan and then spread.
3. Freeze the berry mixture for at least 30 minutes.
4. Take off from the freezer and with a fork, stir the granita thoroughly.
5. Freeze for 2-3 hours, stirring every 30 minutes with a fork.

Avocado & Banana Mousse

Servings|4   Time|15 minutes
Nutritional Content (per serving):
Cal| 302   Fat| 12.1g   Protein| 2.6g   Carbs| 45.2g   Fibre| 7g

Ingredients:

- ❖ 3 medium bananas, peeled & cut up
- ❖ 2 g (1 tsp.) lime zest, grated finely
- ❖ 120 ml (½ C.) fresh lime juice
- ❖ 115 g (1/3 C.) raw honey
- ❖ 2 ripe avocados, peeled, pitted & cut up
- ❖ 2 g (1 tsp.) lemon zest, grated finely
- ❖ 120 ml (½ C.) fresh lemon juice

Directions:

1. Put the bananas and remnant ingredients into an electric blender and process to form a smooth mixture.
2. Transfer the mousse in 4 serving glasses and put into your fridge to chill for around 3-4 hours.

Chocolaty Avocado Pudding

Servings|6   Time|10 minutes
Nutritional Content (per serving):
Cal| 221   Fat| 14.1g   Protein| 2.8g   Carbs| 24.2g   Fibre| 5.9g

Ingredients:
- 2 ripe avocados, peeled, pitted & cut up
- 60 g (½ C.) cacao powder
- ¾ g (¼ tsp.) powdered ancho chile
- 10 ml (2 tsp.) organic vanilla extract
- 120 ml (½ C.) unsweetened almond milk
- 2½ g (1 tsp.) powdered cinnamon
- 115 g (1/3 C.) raw honey

Directions:
1. Put the avocados and remnant ingredients into an electric blender and process to form a smooth mixture.
2. Transfer the mousse into serving glasses and put into your fridge to chill for around 3 hours.

Strawberry Soufflé

Servings|6   Time|30 minutes
Nutritional Content (per serving):
Cal| 100   Fat| 0.3g   Protein| 3.7g   Carbs| 22.2g   Fibre| 2.3g

Ingredients:
- 510 g (18 oz.) fresh strawberries, hulled
- 5 egg whites, divided
- 115 g (1/3 C.) raw honey, divided
- 20 ml (4 tsp.) fresh lemon juice

Directions:
1. For preheating: set your oven at 175 °C (350 °F).
2. Put the strawberries into an electric blender and process to form a puree.
3. Through a strainer, strain the puree.
4. Put the strawberry puree, half of honey, 2 egg whites and lemon juice into a basin and whisk to form a frothy and light mixture. Put the remnant egg whites into another basin and whisk until it is frothy.
5. While whisking gradually put the remnant honey and whisk to form stiff peaks.
6. Gently fold the egg whites into strawberry mixture.
7. Transfer the mixture into six large-sized ramekins.
8. Arrange the ramekins into a baking tray.
9. Bake for around 10-12 minutes.
10. Take off from oven and enjoy right away.

Brown Rice Pudding

Servings|4   Time|1 hour 25 minutes
Nutritional Content (per serving):
Cal| 241   Fat| 10.1g   Protein| 5.3g   Carbs| 31.4g   Fibre| 2.2g

Ingredients:

- 105 g (½ C.) brown rice, soaked for 15 minutes & drained
- 35 g (¼ C.) unsalted cashews
- 1¼ g (½ tsp.) powdered cinnamon, divided
- 25 g (¼ C.) unsalted almonds, cut up
- 360 ml (1½ C.) filtered water
- 600 ml (2½ C.) unsweetened almond milk
- 40 g (2 tbsp.) pure maple syrup
- Pinch of sea salt

Directions:

1. Put the rice and water into a large-sized pot on burner at around medium-high heat.
2. Cook the mixture until boiling.
3. Turn the heat around medium.
4. Cook for around 30 minutes, stirring from time to time.
5. In the meantime, put the almond milk and cashews into an electric blender and process to form a smooth mixture.
6. Slowly put the milk mixture into the pot of rice, stirring all the time.
7. Blend in maple syrup, half of cinnamon and salt and cook for around 30-40 minutes, stirring from time to time.
8. Take off the pot of rice pudding from the burner and set aside to cool slightly.
9. Transfer the rice pudding into serving dishes and sprinkle each with remnant cinnamon.
10. Enjoy moderately hot with the garnishing of almonds.

Beans Brownies

Servings|12 Time|45 minutes
Nutritional Content (per serving):
Cal| 216   Fat| 2.2g   Protein| 9g   Carbs| 43.2g   Fibre| 8g

Ingredients:

- 340 g (2 C.) cooked unsalted black beans
- 30 g (2 tbsp.) almond butter
- 15 g (2 tbsp.) gluten-free quick rolled oats
- 30 g (¼ C.) cacao powder
- 12 Medjool dates, pitted & cut up
- 30 g (2 tbsp.) almond butter
- 10 ml (2 tsp.) organic vanilla extract
- 5 g (2 tsp.) powdered cinnamon

Directions:

1. For preheating: set your oven at 175 °C (350 °F).
2. Lay out bakery paper into a baking pan.
3. Put the beans and remnant ingredients except the cacao powder and cinnamon into an electric food processor and process to form a smooth mixture.
4. Transfer the mixture into a large-sized basin.
5. Put the cacao powder and cinnamon and blend incorporate.
6. Now, transfer the mixture into the baking pan and with the back of a spatula, smooth the top surface.
7. Bake for around 30 minutes.
8. Take off from oven and place onto a wire rack to cool thoroughly.
9. Cut into equal-sized brownies and enjoy.

Chickpea Fudge

Servings|10 Time|15 minutes
Nutritional Content (per serving):
Cal| 92 Fat| 2.4g Protein| 4.7g Carbs| 14.8g Fibre| 5.7g

Ingredients:

- ❖ 330 g (2 C.) cooked unsalted chickpeas
- ❖ 120 g (½ C.) almond butter
- ❖ 5 ml (1 tsp.) organic vanilla extract
- ❖ 8 Medjool dates, pitted & cut up
- ❖ 120 ml (½ C.) unsweetened almond milk
- ❖ 15 g (2 tbsp.) cacao powder

Directions:

1. Lay out bakery paper into a baking pan.
2. Put the chickpeas and remnant ingredients except for cacao powder into an electric food processor and process to incorporate thoroughly.
3. Transfer the mixture into a large-sized basin and blend in cacao powder.
4. Transfer the mixture into the baking pan and smooth the surface with the back of a spatula.
5. Put into your fridge for around 2 hours.
6. Cut into desired sized squares and enjoy.

Blueberry Crumble

Servings|5 Time|55 minutes
Nutritional Content (per serving):
Cal| 129 Fat| 6.4g Protein| 2g Carbs| 16.8g Fibre| 2.7g

Ingredients:

- ❖ Olive oil baking spray
- ❖ 3 g (¾ tsp.) baking soda
- ❖ 30 ml (2 tbsp.) olive oil
- ❖ 45 ml (3 tbsp.) filtered water
- ❖ 225 g (1½ C.) fresh blueberries
- ❖ 045 g (½ C.) gluten-free oat flour
- ❖ 60 g (¼ C.) unripe banana, peeled & mashed
- ❖ 10 ml (2 tsp.) fresh lemon juice

Directions:

1. For preheating: set your oven at 150 °C (300 °F).
2. Lightly spray an 8x8-inch baking pan with baking spray.
3. Put the oat flour and remnant ingredients except the blueberries into a large-sized basin and blend to incorporate thoroughly.
4. Put the blueberries in the bottom of the baking pan and top with flour mixture.
5. Bake for around 40 minutes.
6. Enjoy moderately hot.

30 DAY MEAL PLAN

WEEK 1: Blood Sugar Stabilization & Adrenal Support

Day 1

- ⏱ **Breakfast:** Yoghurt & Berries Bowl
- 🥗 **Lunch:** Citrus Greens Salad
- ☕ **Drink:** Citrus Detox Water
- 🍲 **Dinner:** Turkey & Cabbage Soup
- 🍪 **Snack:** Cinnamon Almonds

Day 2

- ⏱ **Breakfast:** Overnight Oatmeal
- 🥗 **Lunch:** Tuna Sandwiches
- ☕ **Drink:** Chilled Green Tea
- 🍲 **Dinner:** Chicken & Spinach Stew
- 🍪 **Snack:** Sweet Potato Fries

Day 3

- ⏱ **Breakfast:** Apple Omelet
- 🥗 **Lunch:** Egg & Avocado Salad
- ☕ **Drink:** Lemonade
- 🍲 **Dinner:** Cod & Mushroom Casserole
- 🍪 **Snack:** Deviled Eggs

Day 4

- ⏱ **Breakfast:** Fruity Green Smoothie Bowl
- 🥗 **Lunch:** Chickpea Lettuce Wraps
- ☕ **Drink:** Ginger & Lime Herbal Tea
- 🍲 **Dinner:** Orange Poached Salmon
- 🍪 **Snack:** Spiced Chickpeas

Day 5

- ⏱ **Breakfast:** Flaxseed Meal Porridge
- 🥗 **Lunch:** Bulgur Salad
- ☕ **Drink:** Blueberry & Cucumber Smoothie
- 🍲 **Dinner:** Lentil & Rice Bake
- 🍪 **Snack:** Avocado Guacamole

Day 6

- **Breakfast:** Blueberry Muffins
- **Lunch:** Chicken Kabobs
- **Drink:** Elderberry Herbal Tea
- **Dinner:** Turkey & Beans Chili
- **Snack:** Stuffed Cherry Tomatoes

Day 7

- **Breakfast:** Oats & Buckwheat Granola
- **Lunch:** Shrimp in Citrus Sauce
- **Drink:** Lemon Iced Tea
- **Dinner:** Chickpeas & Courgette Curry
- **Snack:** Apple Chips

WEEK 2: Gut Healing & Nutrient Boosting

Day 8

- **Breakfast:** Salmon & Spinach Scramble
- **Lunch:** Stuffed Capsicums
- **Drink:** Apple & Spinach Juice
- **Dinner:** Chicken in Dill Sauce
- **Snack:** Berries Gazpacho

Day 9

- **Breakfast:** Vanilla Pancakes
- **Lunch:** Turkey Koftas
- **Drink:** Kale & Avocado Smoothie
- **Dinner:** Ground Turkey with Lentils
- **Snack:** Spinach Chips

Day 10

- **Breakfast:** Nuts, Seeds & Chia Porridge
- **Lunch:** Sweet Potato Soup
- **Drink:** Chamomile Herbal Tea
- **Dinner:** Shrimp Casserole
- **Snack:** Strawberry Salsa

Day 11

- **Breakfast:** Carrot Bread
- **Lunch:** Chicken Stuffed Avocado
- **Drink:** Strawberry & Orange Smoothie
- **Dinner:** Salmon with Yoghurt Sauce
- **Snack:** Apple Chips

Day 12

- **Breakfast:** Blueberry Waffles
- **Lunch:** Carrot Soup
- **Drink:** Lemon Iced Tea
- **Dinner:** Barley & Lentil Stew
- **Snack:** Deviled Eggs

Day 13

- **Breakfast:** Overnight Seeds Porridge
- **Lunch:** Scallops in Yoghurt Sauce
- **Drink:** Citrus Detox Water
- **Dinner:** Chicken & Cauliflower Curry
- **Snack:** Cinnamon Almonds

Day 14

- **Breakfast:** Veggies Frittata
- **Lunch:** Egg Drop Soup
- **Drink:** Orange Juice
- **Dinner:** Turkey & Mushroom Bake
- **Snack:** Stuffed Cherry Tomatoes

WEEK 3: Deep Cortisol Repair & Hormonal Stability

Day 15

- **Breakfast:** Quinoa Porridge
- **Lunch:** Salmon Burgers
- **Drink:** Apple & Spinach Juice
- **Dinner:** Turkey & Beans Chili
- **Snack:** Apple Chips

Day 16

🥣 **Breakfast:** Flaxseed Meal Porridge
🥗 **Lunch:** Stuffed Capsicums
🍵 **Drink:** Ginger & Lime Herbal Tea
🍲 **Dinner:** Chicken in Dill Sauce
🍪 **Snack:** Deviled Eggs

Day 17

🥣 **Breakfast:** Overnight Seeds Porridge
🥗 **Lunch:** Carrot Soup
🍵 **Drink:** Blueberry & Cucumber Smoothie
🍲 **Dinner:** Lentil & Rice Bake
🍪 **Snack:** Stuffed Cherry Tomatoes

Day 18

🥣 **Breakfast:** Blueberry Muffins
🥗 **Lunch:** Chicken Kabobs
🍵 **Drink:** Strawberry Detox Water
🍲 **Dinner:** Salmon with Yoghurt Sauce
🍪 **Snack:** Cinnamon Almonds

Day 19

🥣 **Breakfast:** Nuts, Seeds & Chia Porridge
🥗 **Lunch:** Chickpea Lettuce Wraps
🍵 **Drink:** Kale & Avocado Smoothie
🍲 **Dinner:** Chicken & Cauliflower Curry
🍪 **Snack:** Spiced Chickpeas

Day 20

🥣 **Breakfast:** Vanilla Pancakes
🥗 **Lunch:** Citrus Greens Salad
🍵 **Drink:** Lemon Iced Tea
🍲 **Dinner:** Barley & Lentil Stew
🍪 **Snack:** Avocado Guacamole

Day 21

- 🥣 **Breakfast:** Oats & Buckwheat Granola
- 🥗 **Lunch:** Turkey Koftas
- ☕ **Drink:** Elderberry Herbal Tea
- 🍽 **Dinner:** Orange Poached Salmon
- 🥮 **Snack:** Sweet Potato Fries

WEEK 4: Optimizing Energy & Restorative Sleep

Day 22

- 🥣 **Breakfast:** Yoghurt & Berries Bowl
- 🥗 **Lunch:** Egg & Avocado Salad
- ☕ **Drink:** Chilled Green Tea
- 🍽 **Dinner:** Ground Turkey with Lentils
- 🥮 **Snack:** Berries Gazpacho

Day 23

- 🥣 **Breakfast:** Apple Omelet
- 🥗 **Lunch:** Shrimp in Citrus Sauce
- ☕ **Drink:** Strawberry & Orange Smoothie
- 🍽 **Dinner:** Chickpeas & Courgette Curry
- 🥮 **Snack:** Spinach Chips

Day 24

- 🥣 **Breakfast:** Carrot Bread
- 🥗 **Lunch:** Sweet Potato Soup
- ☕ **Drink:** Lemonade
- 🍽 **Dinner:** Turkey & Mushroom Bake
- 🥮 **Snack:** Strawberry Salsa

Day 25

- 🥣 **Breakfast:** Fruity Green Smoothie Bowl
- 🥗 **Lunch:** Scallops in Yoghurt Sauce
- ☕ **Drink:** Citrus Detox Water
- 🍽 **Dinner:** Chicken & Spinach Stew
- 🥮 **Snack:** Apple Chips

Day 26

🍳 **Breakfast:** Salmon & Spinach Scramble
🍲 **Lunch:** Tuna Sandwiches
🥤 **Drink:** Apple & Spinach Juice
🍲 **Dinner:** Cod & Mushroom Casserole
🥧 **Snack:** Deviled Eggs

Day 27

🍳 **Breakfast:** Blueberry Waffles
🍲 **Lunch:** Bulgur Salad
🥤 **Drink:** Ginger & Lime Herbal Tea
🍲 **Dinner:** Turkey & Cabbage Soup
🥧 **Snack:** Stuffed Cherry Tomatoes

Day 28

🍳 **Breakfast:** Overnight Oatmeal
🍲 **Lunch:** Chicken Stuffed Avocado
🥤 **Drink:** Strawberry & Orange Smoothie
🍲 **Dinner:** Shrimp Casserole
🥧 **Snack:** Cinnamon Almonds

Day 29

🍳 **Breakfast:** Veggies Frittata
🍲 **Lunch:** Egg Drop Soup
🥤 **Drink:** Chamomile Herbal Tea
🍲 **Dinner:** Chicken in Dill Sauce
🥧 **Snack:** Apple Chips

Day 30

🍳 **Breakfast:** Quinoa Porridge
🍲 **Lunch:** Turkey Koftas
🥤 **Drink:** Kale & Avocado Smoothie
🍲 **Dinner:** Lentil & Rice Bake
🥧 **Snack:** Berries Gazpacho

Thank You for Joining Me on This Journey

You've made it to the end of **The Ultimate Cortisol Diet Plan Recipe Book**, but really, this is just the **beginning of your journey** toward balanced hormones, better energy, and a more vibrant, stress-free life.

I hope this book has given you **the tools, knowledge, and delicious recipes** to nourish your body and support your adrenal health. More importantly, I hope it has helped you **feel more in control of your well-being** and given you the confidence to make food choices that truly support your health.

Your Feedback Means the World! 🫶

If you enjoyed this book, found it helpful, or simply loved trying out the recipes, I would be incredibly grateful if you could **take a moment to leave a review**.

📖 **Why Your Review Matters:**
✔ It helps **others who are struggling with high cortisol** discover this book and get the support they need.
✔ Your feedback allows me to **continue creating valuable content** to help people just like you.
✔ It truly means the world to me to hear about **your experience and success stories!**

☀ **Leaving a review is simple and only takes a minute, but it makes a HUGE difference!**

Printed in Great Britain
by Amazon

59659748R00051